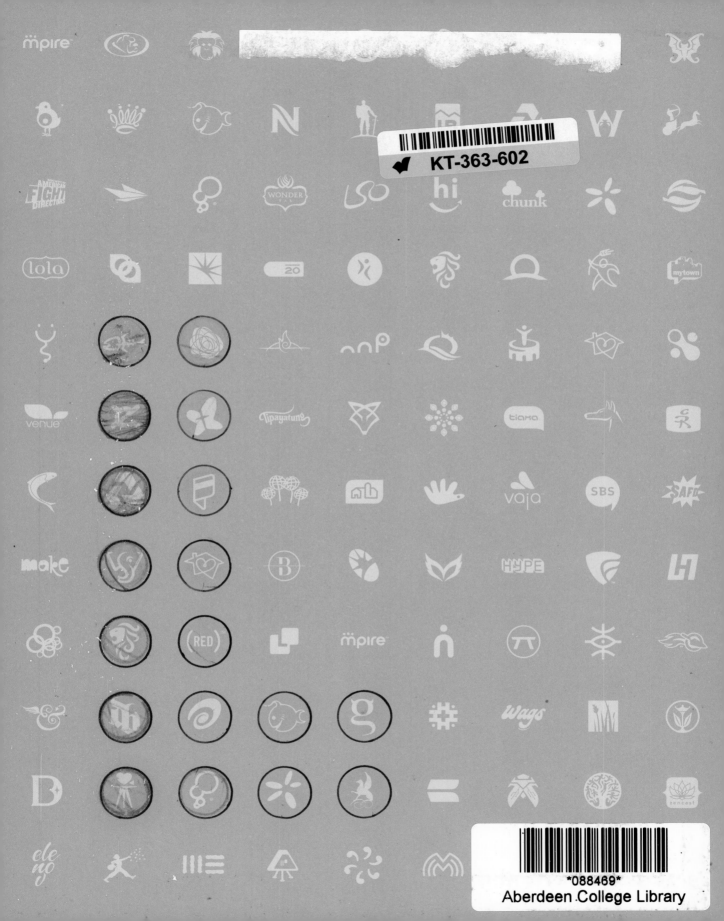

DESIGN MATTERS //

# LOGOS 01

AN ESSENTIAL PRIMER FOR TODAY'S COMPETITIVE MARKET          CAPSULE

ROCKPORT

First published in the United States of America by
Rockport Publishers, a member of
Quayside Publishing Group
33 Commercial Street
Gloucester, Massachusetts 01930-5089
Telephone: (978) 282-9590
Fax: (978) 283-2742
www.rockpub.com

**Library of Congress Cataloging-in-Publication Data**
Logos 01 : an essential primer for today's competitive market /
[design], Capsule.
    p.  cm.– (Design matters)
  ISBN-13: 978-1-59253-341-1
  ISBN-10: 1-59253-341-8
  1. Logos (Symbols)–Design.  I. Capsule (Firm) II. Title: Logos zero one.
  NC1002.L63L656 2007
  741.6–dc22                              2006035929
                                               CIP

ISBN-13: 978-1-59253-341-1
ISBN-10: 1-59253-341-8


10 9 8 7 6 5 4 3 2 1

Design: CAPSULE
10 South 5th Street, Suite 645
Minneapolis, Minnesota 55402
USA
612-341-4525
www.capsule.us


Printed in China

WITHDRAWN

# Contents

# INTROD

# UCTION

TO FULFILL A DREAM, TO BE ALLOWED TO
SWEAT OVER LONELY LABOR, TO BE GIVEN
THE CHANCE TO CREATE, IS THE MEAT AND
POTATOES OF LIFE. THE MONEY IS THE
GRAVY.  – BETTE DAVIS, *THE LONELY LIFE*

THE WALLPAPER OF SPANISH CAVEMEN, THE HIEROGLYPH-RIDDEN OBELISKS OF ANCIENT EGYPT– MODERN LOGOS DESCEND FROM A PRIMEVAL TRADITION OF ICONOGRAPHY, EMBODYING THE SAME SIMPLICITY, DIRECTNESS, AND PREOCCUPATION WITH VISUAL CODIFICATION HUMANS EMBRACED LONG, LONG AGO.

# What Is a Logo?

Just as ancient ancestors communicated through visual icons, modern brands speak to customers through imagery. Brands use logos to impress values, functions, and hierarchies on millions of people. Design one, and you have the responsibility and opportunity to make a lasting global impression.

Visual icons communicate basically and directly—which is perfect for branding, when the goal is to convey a message with minimum time or strain on the audience. This is not to say words aren't important, especially for more evolved forms of communication, such as, say, novels or inauguration speeches. These benefit greatly from well-bred vocabularies. Logo design, however, is about cutting the message to the quick.

This book aspires to inform anyone who has joined or wants to join the great tradition of long-gone cavemen and Egyptians. It's for designers hoping to make a unique mark on the canvas of time, presenting theories, process, examples, and methods from design professionals around the world. It's structured to guide readers through the defined stages of process: planning, creating, and implementing. The book also delves into the abstract, emotional, and instinctual elements that are so critical to creativity of any kind.

# Why Are Logos Created?

## A LOGO IS WORTH A THOUSAND WORDS

If you grew up with a houseful of siblings or ever had a college roommate with a penchant for "borrowing" clothes, you know the value of a good Sharpie marker. Why, with two little initials, you can take passive-aggressive control of all your worldly possessions, one thick, black scrawl at a time. Logos are like Sharpie markers for brands. They tell everyone which brand owns which product, service, or communications vehicle. This is a Nike shoe. That is a FedEx box. This is a Pepsi billboard. Logos identify ownership, first and foremost, and often end up doing much more.

Today, the world bustles with roughly 5,000-plus written or spoken languages. Beyond those, there is an even larger array of visual languages that communicate even more efficiently. Across this communications offering, logos are a virtually universal tool. They communicate information about the sender, the medium, and the recipient. Take an orange from the grocery store, for example. The sender is a farmer in Spain, the medium is the orange, and the recipient is someone seeking a sweet source of vitamin C. All three have an interest in the orange's little sticker label icon, benefiting from it in disparate but related ways. That icon tethers all three together. By marking the fruit, the brand takes possession of the fruit. By choosing the fruit with a particular logo, the recipient takes possession of the brand.

Logos send messages of all sorts to mixed audiences. They shorten the communication of a complex statement to something simple, clear, and concise. They replace written language when audiences don't have the time or will to read. You'll never find a label on an orange that states "this is a farm-fresh orange from Spain that is safe for you to eat until later this month." Instead, that orange bears the Nadal label. When consumers see that, they know the orange is fresh from Spain.

The orange example outlines how a commodity product gains depth and communicates information through its logo. The following explores how logos can add value to a specialty product and then aid in clearly communicating that value.

THIS IS A FARM-FRESH ORANGE FROM SPAIN THAT IS SAFE FOR YOU TO EAT UNTIL LATER THIS MONTH

*A logo most often consists of either type and a visual shape or form, or just type, as in a logotype. The Red Wing Shoes' logo is unique, in that the old logo doesn't allow the type and shape to exist separately.*

## RED WING SHOES: ONE CENTURY, ONE WING

Red Wing Shoes, a U.S. manufacturer, has a premium reputation that has endured for more than a century and has spread worldwide. Its name and its logo, a literal image of a red wing, are inspired by the brand's birthplace.

Red Wing Shoes was established in Red Wing, Minnesota, in 1905. Since then, the once small-town operation has gathered admirers from places as far-flung as Europe and Asia. The logo is not only a symbol of a shoe company, it is a link between Red Wing, the brand, and Red Wing, the town. The logo represents their shared history, values, and participants.

Red Wing's story is an example of a brand, history, and logo working together in synergy. This balance is the primary reason Red Wing Shoes has become so popular around the world. When foreign consumers buy Red Wing Shoes' products, they are embracing quality and reliability, but most important, they are tasting a genuine slice of Americana.

*A red-dyed swan wing is the inspiration for Chief Red Wing's name, Hanapahupata. The wing is also the inspiration for a high-quality work boot from Minnesota, USA.*

# Visual Translation

## LOGO IS A FOUR-LETTER IDEA

Design blossomed from architecture, a craft that evolved into a profession. Since then, the term "design" has been adopted by almost every professional field, from engineering to advertising to technology. The reason for this is most certainly because the very definition of the word "design" is so ambiguous. Like water or air, the concept of design is so elemental that it can slink silently into the backdrop of virtually every scene.

One area in which design boldly takes center stage is the graphic design industry. Hence, with the focus on design, the key player is the designer. And the key driver is the graphic designer's perspective. Ideally, graphic designers have a passion, not only for the creative aspects of design but also for the discipline of design— the organization, codification, and propagation of information and ideas.

The designer should understand that design is not in the final logo design. That is the end product of design. Design is an action, an experiential medley of stages and ideas that spackle the void between what is conceived and what truly is.

Graphic design's function is visual communication of a message through form and structure for a specified audience, as broad or specific as the client requires. A logo design visually represents brands in marketplaces. The result should be a logo design that not only translates the brand but also does it quickly and memorably for the audience.

Just how influential is a logo? Can a great logo make a great company? A logo is a powerful weapon. It can boost consumer perception. It can boost internal perception. What a logo cannot do is actually make the company great. It can and should be the flag that signals brand change. An example of this is the amazingly effective pull of McDonalds. Children too young to read brighten at the sight of its golden arches dawning on the interstate horizon—they get the message.

Look back at the history of century-old brands. You'll see how a brand's logo change runs parallel to changes in its business strategy. But it bears repeating: a great logo does not create a great brand or organization. The logo is a flag. The guts of a brand reside in the consistent qualities and values of the people in the organization.

# mamamoto

*A simple logotype is the logo design's core.
The gender-neutral script evokes elegance
and modernity.* LIGALUX

*The logo design expands into an elegantly
complex visual system, representing
everything from toys and buttons to the
organization's manifesto.*

## REDESIGNING HOW WE SEE THE FAMILY

The Mamamoto manifesto calls for an end to cute bears and fussy floral patterns in children's fashion. Mamamoto has a simple goal. It seeks to change how
we, as a global society, overwhelmingly associate children with simple images,
instead of more complex, intelligent, or visually interesting designs.

The Mamamoto logo design channels the core idea of kid-friendly sophistication
from simple logotype to a larger system. It visually energizes the brand, creating
an interesting, intelligent, and complex visual language that is unique in the
world of children's fashion.

# Brands Tell Stories

## A BEGINNING, A LOGO, AND A BRAND

Great storytellers don't just read out loud. They evoke. Great storytellers build fright with eyebrows, ignite suspense through timing, and punch walls with voice. When a brand tells a story, it too employs tools to gain the ear of its audience. Today, these tools explore far beyond the realms of traditional advertising. New storytelling tools are growing more and more diverse, subversive, and surprising. Logos are more important then ever, because they make sure the brand is still connected to the story. In a world where integrated marketing communications are trampling advertising's outmoded methods, logos are an essential linking agent.

All brands tell stories. Colleges, supermodels, theme parks, grocery stores, even cities and states, all own brands. Everyone and everything has something to say. It's the way in which they say it that shapes the relationship with audiences. The goal is first to communicate a relevant, consistent message. Then, it's living up to the message through the behaviors of employees and stakeholders.

Consumer brands speak through advertising, the Internet, and packaging. Business brands converse with audiences through a sales force, literature, and the Internet. Each medium contributes beyond the intended message. For example, a phone number on a business card carries different baggage than that same number etched on a bathroom stall. It's not just what's said, but how and where it's said.

Brands and books both tell stories. If a brand were a book, for example, the logo would be the cover. It's the glossy, embossed visual finger coyly beckoning the consumer. It's no wonder brand managers spend so much time and resources ensuring that a logo communicates the intended message. Advertising campaigns change, key messages change, and even brand managers change, but, if it's working hard, a logo design often stays the same for many years.

Because a logo appears so often and in so many places, its message must be clear, refined, and protected. If your logo is speaking to your audiences, what is it saying? What do the colors say about your brand? What does the shape say? What does the type say? All of these pieces come together to speak in a visual language about your brand. Is it what you intended? If not, what are you doing to change the language of your logo?

*A logotype's simplicity doesn't require anything more to communicate an idea's essence. With only one number and four letters, the message is clear.* PENTAGRAM

*A logo design must excel in the place where it will be seen most often. Often, a magazine logo is also a visually identifiable masthead.*

## *2WICE*: STRAIGHT TWO THE ART

*2wice* is an arts journal, published twice a year. The limited number of issues allows the publisher to delve acutely into targeted artistic subject areas, as each issue focuses on a single fine art medium: film, fashion, design, performance, etc. For the publisher, the result is clarity and focus. For the reader, the breadth and quality of the writing is well worth the wait.

The logo design for *2wice* needed to identify the unique qualities of this nonprofit arts organization, alluding to its diverse interests and passions. It also had to work in all situations like a brand ambassador, bowing to accommodate different communication scenarios.

# PLANN

NG

JUST BECAUSE SOMETHING DOESN'T DO
WHAT YOU PLANNED IT TO DO DOESN'T
MEAN IT'S USELESS.  – THOMAS EDISON

MAPS COME IN ALL FORMS. DIGITAL NAVIGATION SPEAKS TO DRIVERS. OLD PHOTOS AND SCRAPS OF PAPER ILLUMINATE THE PATH TO DEEPLY HIDDEN MEMORIES. SETTING STRATEGY IS A PROCESS OF SKETCHING THE MAP, WHETHER YOU BASE ITS CREATION ON LOGIC OR INSTINCT. THE REALLY GOOD ONES LEAD TO TREASURE.

# Setting Strategy

Setting strategy is all about understanding what you have to say and to whom you have to say it. If a company wants to base strategy on price, it should say it is the best value, and it should say it to people for whom value is the most important selling point. Storewide sales can be a profitable selling tool for these companies, especially in generic product categories.

Of course, another strategy is to emphasize unique qualities that make a brand desirable, regardless of price. This way, the brand can attract consumers without having to cut into profit. Classic brand strategy engages the consumer thought process by designing emotional benefits into brands. By tying emotion to the brand, brand strategy meets the consumer's emotional requirements while leaving price, availability, purpose, and other features and benefits to satisfy rational needs.

Logos are an important part of this equation. Logos help consumers make decisions by embodying the meaning of the brand, spreading the most desirable attributes in front of the consumer and making the decision identifiable and easy.

Brand strategy is all about finding the path to earning customer loyalty, increasing margins, and keeping customers coming back day after day. The following section explores ways to set strategy.

# The Reasons We Ask Questions

WHO SAYS SUPERMODELS ARE DUMB?

Which came first: the answer or the question? Unlike that vexatious chicken and egg, the answer to this riddle is fairly straightforward. Questions—What's the meaning of life? Is there a heaven? Where's the other sock?—can and do exist without clear-cut answers. However, answers—"happiness," "maybe," and "in the dryer"—cannot be uncovered without first asking a question. This applies to planning strategy. The more questions, the more answers. The more answers, the stronger and more relevant the consequent design.

Sometimes designers must set their own business strategy, as is the case for many freelancers. Sometimes they just need to be able to communicate with account people. What exactly do you know about business?

To learn a little more, gather and organize your questions. Then take the list and go to the nearest sphere of business thinking, be it the "business" section of the library, the bookstore, or the Internet. Don't waste time with reheated strategy. Get answers from the leaders of the pack.

If you're a designer creating a business strategy, it's good to read up on modern business thinkers such as David Aaker, Peter Drucker, and Michael Porter. There are plenty of authors to pick from, and it's not difficult material. Like most business strategy, their work is straightforward and fairly easy for beginners to understand. You might find it dry at first, but eventually you can start to connect it back to your world and apply it in your daily client work.

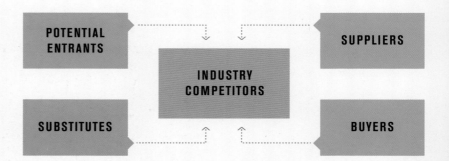

*Porter's Five Forces model, a simple tool that frames industry power dynamics, is just one of countless business tools that can help focus design toward the client's business objectives. The Porter's Five Forces model identifies market forces that impact the client's business.*

Even designers who have the benefit of account people should maintain a certain level of business strategy in their own right. With it, you can better showcase the power of your design to business audiences. This will strengthen the case to any business manager at any level of any organization.

For PrairieStone Pharmacy, a new entrant into the highly competitive medical category, business strategy was a key driver of the brand strategy. Part of the company's business strategy was to recruit a quality workforce by offering a better work environment for pharmacists, employees who are hard to find in a competitive market. One way PrairieStone improved the work environment was by introducing automated pill-sorting technology that allowed pharmacists to get out from behind the glass wall.

A peripheral benefit of this was that functional space behind the counter could be reduced, lowering the cost of operations and increasing profit per retail square foot. This in turn attracted retail clients who planned to add a pharmacy to their retail operations—they were drawn to PrairieStone's service quality and ability, consistently, to increase overall store traffic. These dynamics helped strengthen a powerful and valuable business strategy that led to a thoughtful brand strategy. These strategies then informed a logo design that exemplified the PrairieStone Pharmacy story. Understanding the business strategy made the design stronger and more relevant.

*Early pharmacies in the Midwest region of the United States used prairie stone to create mortars and pestles. PrairieStone Pharmacy's logo functions nationally while alluding to its agrarian roots.* CAPSULE

Design as a discipline is a competitive advantage. It's a fundamental part of the business strategy. Therefore, citizens of any design community need to believe in business strategy and understand it before they begin designing.

# Purpose of Planning

## DON'T TICK OFF THE CLOCK

"I do my best work under pressure." Ever heard that? Ever said that? It's the credo of procrastinators everywhere. We'd all like to think that great work is the product of ingenious, "Eureka!" moments, when lightning strikes and creations miraculously spring forth. This is risky. Even if procrastination has worked in the past, a happy fluke does not a modus operandi make.

## One hour of planning usually eliminates two hours of reworking. Plan now and enjoy extra time later.

Beware—or, before you know it, you're holding a snarling deadline at bay with nothing but a mocha-fueled all-nighter and a presentation riddled with more holes than Grandma's latest crochet project. As for that "work under pressure" nonsense? Pure poppycock. Your thrown-together presentation may very well be better than another person's well-planned presentation. Fine. But your thrown-together presentation will never be better than your own well-planned presentation. If you want to progress as a designer, plan in advance and check excuses at the door.

Also, keep in mind that success is not synonymous with perfection. Planning never removes all risk. In many organizations, strategic planning constitutes hours of meetings spent setting strategies and tactics. It can become easy to worry over little details of the planning effort and rigidly follow the rules. But a successful plan is gauged by big-picture success. When you encounter bumps in the road, simply adapt the plan. The more bumps you encounter, the more proof there is that a definitive plan was in place to begin with. Don't get tangled up in execution. Keep your eye on the big prize.

*The copper logo signals the quality of each Outset product. The logo offers trademark protection and is highly valuable when facing international competitors offering much lower prices and qualities.* OUTSET, INC. WITH AKA CREATIVE.

## THE OUTSET BRAND: RARE DESIGN, DONE WELL

"Foodies" are a growing force in the marketplace. They are mostly baby boomers who view the creation and enjoyment of cuisine as a refined hobby. "Grill masters" are a particularly passionate subset within this category. Seasoned grill masters are concerned with three things: the quality of the grill, the meat, and the tools.

The Outset brand increases the impact of its mark by making it a primary focus of the product design. In traditional execution, the logo is part of the packaging, which is discarded soon after purchase. Or it is a small mark on a corner of the product, to be seen or ignored at the user's discretion. Outset made the logo a primary focal point of its products, so users are reminded of exactly what brand they are using every time they grill, wash, or put away their grilling utensils.

*The logo becomes part of the product as a simplified graphic element. It pleases aesthetically and provides a point of conversation between the grill master and the grill master's friends and family.*

# Creating the Ideal Logo Design Brief

KEEP YOUR EYES ON THE ROAD

Design briefs: keep them brief. Seems simple enough to remember, no? It may be simple to remember, but lassoing 100 years of a business, three months of current research, and a gaggle of planning meetings into one brief document is a formidable task—and this will often be the case. Keep design briefs brief, to the point, and easy to follow.

Beyond being spare, design briefs must set direction and inspire design. So the more focused the language, the better. And the more inspirational the language, the better. Start preparing the brief by defining brand strategy. From there, pinpoint the brand's core competitors, collaborators, and customers.

Once you identify the basics, set expectations. Write with precise, thoughtful language. Communicate the final objectives and goals with a rich (but concise) explanation that properly sets client expectations. Establish a wide variety of objectives concerning components that are measurable: timing, budget, sales, etc. But also remind the client that, though

creative goals aren't necessarily quantifiable, they are observable and just as important. If only measurable objectives are set forth, then those are the only objectives by which the work is judged, irrespective of other accomplishments.

Successful briefs don't just set expectations, they also translate. The brief is the bridge between the thought and the image, so it must be descriptive. Therefore, language is essential—the more illustrative, the better. For example, what does the frequently encountered word "innovative" really mean? What is the visual association? Does it translate visually? Not necessarily. Dynamic words don't always make dynamic visuals. A better way to create visual associations is to reference existing images or abstract iterations. Spend time experimenting and figuring out which visual option works best.

The design brief should also consider and answer the classic *whos* and *whats*. Who is the client (history, people, size, and industry)? What are the budget and timeline (overall

and broken down piece by piece)? Who is the audience (age, income, location, habits, and tastes)? What has occurred to date? What is the catalyst for changing the logo, and what has been done so far? What does success look like for the client (specific analytical goals, return on investment, sales, usage rates, internal rate of return, or any other predetermined analytical benchmarks)? And, what is the makeup of the decision-making team (people, personalities, individual goals, and a final decision-maker)?

Finally, how much time should it take to create a brief? After all research and strategy work is complete, no more than two hours. If it takes longer, you're likely starting to rehash existing strategy or language. How much time should it take to review a brief? Two hours is bordering on excessive. If you catch yourself admiring the increasingly elaborate doodles of your design team, it's a not-so-subtle sign that things have taken a turn off the productive highway. Boredom is a bad way to kick off a project. Keep the brief clear, focused, and brief.

# DESIGN BRIEF QUESTIONS

••• What three audiences will see this logo design the most often?

••• If there was one thing you could communicate to each audience, what would that be?

••• What are the brand attributes, promises, features, benefits, and positioning statement?

••• What words describe the brand personality? What visuals communicate the brand personality?

••• Where will this logo appear most often? On what media: golf balls; billboards; business cards?

••• Are there any must-haves or nice-to-have items?

••• Who are your competitors? Who are your collaborators?

••• What is the budget in hours? When are presentations scheduled?

••• Why do you need a logo? Or, why are you changing the existing logo design?

••• How will you measure this logo design's success? Smooth implementation? Awards? A change in signals? An energized staff? Other tests or benchmarks?

## AT&T: THE INFLUENCE OF A BRIEF ON AN INTERNATIONAL LOGO REDESIGN

When SBC and AT&T merged, AT&T required a logo to signal significant changes to the business strategy. Ed Whitacre Jr., AT&T's president and CEO, voiced the brand's vision as aiming "to be the only communications and entertainment company our customers will ever want."

Interbrand was asked to design a new entity to help actualize this goal in both business and residential sectors. The firm worked off a design brief based around Whitacre's vision, as well as around anticipated changes to the brand resulting from the merger. Extensive brand research confirmed that AT&T was an internationally recognized, iconic brand with a valuable heritage. But many consumers said the company had disappeared from the residential arena and primarily served business-to-business customers.

The goal was to change the perception of the AT&T brand from the monolithic Ma Bell of the past to an evolved company, by balancing AT&T's innovative heritage with SBC's ability to deliver communications and entertainment.

The creative brief defined the brand's positioning strategy by first defining who the key targets were, what the compelling promise was for both residential and business customers, and why consumers should believe this promise. Guided by the creative brief, research uncovered that, over time, the logo had become attached to negative consumer perceptions. For some consumers, the "death star" globe and bold AT&T type appeared bureaucratic and impersonal.

After deciding to change the globe, the team created logo options ranging from evolutionary treatments to revolutionary transformations. Although they had uncovered negative associations with the old globe, the team also found that the drastically retooled identities were too far removed from the original globe and lost the original brand mark's core value and positive consumer equity.

*Saul Bass designed the original AT&T logo. For years, it adapted smoothly from one medium to the next. After a lifetime of dutiful service, however, the logo began showing age and became bogged down by consumer brand perceptions and other external factors.*
BASS & YAGER

Rather than change the primary color, blue, the designers alluded to modern technology by adding dimension to the globe. The original horizontal wires enveloping the globe symbolized worldwide communications. Updated wires now also impart transparency and luminosity, increasing the brand's approachability and capturing a sense of openness central to the revitalized brand.

Beyond the globe, an even more dramatic change occurred in the logotype. Designers created a custom lowercase font based on the Cingular identity's font, Avenir. Solid monolithic type switched out in favor of softer lowercase type. The resulting tone was more personable, dynamic, and fitting of a business spearheading innovative technology.

*Modern improvements to the classic globe don't detract from existing brand history. They expound upon original visual assets to better reflect internal brand development. The ultimate purpose is to show consumers that significant change is occurring—something has improved.*

INTERBRAND

ONCE UPON A PANCAKE, PEOPLE INSISTED THE WORLD WAS FLAT. THEN SOMEONE DID A LITTLE RESEARCH. WITH JUST A WHIP OF CURIOSITY AND A DAB OF EXPLORATION, THE WORLD SWELLED INTO A ROTUND, COMPLICATED, SOUFFLÉ OF POSSIBILITIES. RESEARCH, IT SEEMS, LITERALLY MADE THE WORLD GO ROUND.

GATHER
ROUND,
EVERYONE

# Conducting Research

A number of things qualify as research. Browsing the Internet. Full, in-depth research, using thousands of individual interviews, months of video analysis, and summary reports stacked on their own dolly. It's all research. Some research methods have a larger price tag, in return for a higher level of confidence in the information they provide. Others offer a much smaller price tag or are completely free. These must be taken for what they are—unregulated and potentially unreliable.

When researching, consider two things. One: know your source. Where does the data come from, and how does the source impact the data received? If you have a research company conducting research, it is part of the source. If you don't trust it, don't use it. Two: conduct enough research to be confident in the results and your opinion of the results. However, also keep in mind that 100 percent confidence doesn't exist.

# What to Research and Why

THE PATH TO KNOWLEDGE IS PAVED WITH SHARP STONES

Drooling with excitement. Nodding in unison. Your team is really getting it. Getting a nap in, that is. Research can be pretty boring business. Unfortunately, it's unavoidable if you want to do a proper job. You'll sift a fair amount of sand before you hit pay dirt. Understanding the three stages, three elements, and many methods of research helps hasten the hunt.

Elements are the things being studied. They always remain the same: people, objects, and culture. People are the individuals whose actions and personalities influence—and are influenced by—the experiences of others. Researchers study people by listening to them and observing behaviors. Objects are the things we interact with every day, the physical devices that impact our lives. Researchers study objects by holding, handling, and dissecting them, then questioning how they affect lives and watching how people interact with them. Finally, culture comprises all the history and patterns that make up the human race. To understand cultures and even subcultures, one must study the history, traditions, and values of the community.

Most important, start by memorizing the three elements: people, objects, and culture. Got it? It's not always that simple. But fundamentally it can be simplified to these three.

Thorough research includes three core stages: exploration, data gathering, and testing. Exploration outlines broad issues surrounding the subject matter or elements being studied. Data gathering is about, well, gathering data. At this point you convert the data into information and eventually to knowledge. Testing is the final stage. It's an interaction between individuals and ideas or concepts, meant to identify issues or create a higher level of confidence.

# smith&nephew

The "burst of energy" symbolizes Smith & Nephew's ongoing passion. The bright, sunny orange sways contrary to most medical product brands, setting the brand apart and conveying warmth and energy. The casual typeface radiates casual friendliness.

WOLFF OLINS

## SMITH & NEPHEW: TEACH AN OLD BRAND NEW TRICKS

Research was essential to Wolff Olins' redesign of Smith & Nephew. When the 150-year-old firm took on several big acquisitions, it required a logo and brand image to reflect its new direction.

Wolff Olins started by gathering common language and beliefs from among Smith & Nephew's various business units around the world. Findings suggested that they were united in one goal: helping patients by "giving them their lives back." This became the simple, elegant, and highly emotional core of Smith & Nephew's brand, from logo design to videos and packing boxes.

Never overlook a moment to make a connection. Even on shipping containers the opportunity exists to communicate a message. Wolff Olins used several media to communicate Smith & Nephew's message.

*Use launch tools to help introduce the brand into employees' lives. This is especially valuable for companies like Smith & Nephew, whose thousands of employees can be leveraged to help spread the brand's story.*

## THE THREE ELEMENTS OF UNDERSTANDING ANY MARKETPLACE

The three research fundamentals are people, objects, and culture. No study can be conducted without influence from these fundamentals. No conclusions can be drawn without understanding how they influence each other. The iPod as a marketplace phenomenon is a good example for illustrating the interdependent relationship among these fundamentals.

### PEOPLE

In simplified terms, the iPod phenomenon involves two sets of people. One group is made up of the individuals who listen to music. The other is made up of the people at Apple who created the iPod.

### OBJECTS

The iPod is one of several objects within the history of mobile music: before it came the boom box, Walkman, and Discman. Understanding the iPod as an object entails looking at it within a historical context.

### CULTURE

Culture includes the belief systems, history, and past patterns of behavior that are the glue holding objects and people together. The iPod blends into behaviors and history surrounding music, commuting, sports, and many other aspects of regional and global culture.

These three elements cannot be separated or substantially defined without one another. Consider all three carefully throughout the research effort. The most common research methods are observation, surveys (print and digital), face-to-face interviews, focus groups, and field studies.

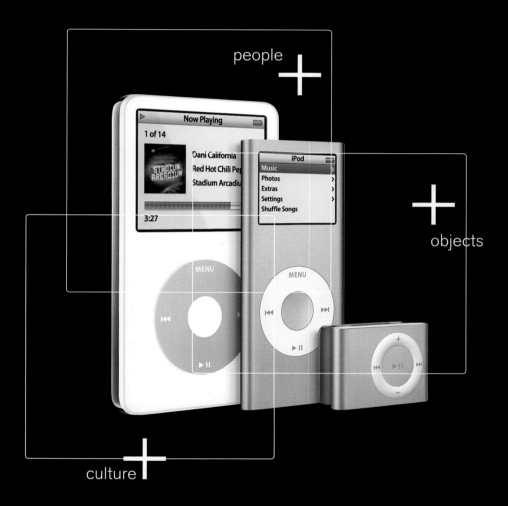

people +

objects +

+ culture

*People, objects, and culture are inextricably interwoven. They cannot be separated or substantially defined without one another. Consider all three carefully throughout the research effort.*

## URBAN LEGEND OR SUBURBAN MYTH?

Pirates no longer sport eye patches. They look like average citizens, looting digital music right from the family computer. Because of this, performers are returning to the road in droves, increasingly relying on live-performance income to supplement shrinking record sales. Leading up to this trend, demand for road venues had been waning for a solid decade, and during that time, not enough locations grew to support current industry needs.

*Engage in primary research. To experience club atmosphere firsthand, the design team traveled to Las Vegas and visited, among others, the club Tangerine.*

Today, intense competition for audiences and demand for space is pulling artists out of traditional music hubs and into the arms of swelling suburban audiences. Myth Nightclub in Minnesota is one of the first to recognize and cater to this trend. Capsule strove to infuse Myth's logo with this innovative spirit.

Myth's founders dreamed of a concert venue rivaling the dazzling boutique clubs of Las Vegas and chose Capsule to design a logo that would help launch a new suburban concert venue with urban appeal. The challenge was to adapt a Las Vegas atmosphere to attract suburban audiences. To capture the client's vision, Capsule needed to develop a business strategy and conduct qualitative research.

Capsule began by splitting the client team into two parts: one undertaking a brand definition process and the other engaged in a visual ideation process. Visual ideation is an important first step because it helps inform and inspire the design team. The process began with brainstorming. The team gathered relevant resources from the worlds of fashion, technology, music, sports, and travel. It then clipped visually intriguing images from each world and filtered them into three style categories. Each category was created on a separate style board that framed the brand visually in a unique way.

The boards accomplished two essential goals: they brought the client directly into the process by setting style, color, and tone, and, most important, they provoked and guided dialogue to answer objectives for the brand.

*Use style boards to articulate a visual language. Style boards, such as these designed for Myth, are especially helpful for soliciting client feedback and creating a common language that both designer and client can understand.* CAPSULE

The group that undertook the brand definition process outlined the brand's personality, functional benefits, features, and key messages for the designers. When both groups were finished, Capsule headed to Vegas to bring the visual ideation and brand together. Primary research, which included face-to-face interviews and artifact gathering, outlined expectations and provided tangible inspiration. Capsule spoke with patrons, club owners, artists, and talent agents, who provided insight into club life from several perspectives. Additionally,

Capsule went into clubs seeking artifacts: menus, matchbooks, flyers, coasters, T-shirts, and more. By collecting paraphernalia with a function or look that said something about its respective club, the team was able to bring home physical items to inspire its work.

The preliminary planning and client exercises were an essential part of achieving a logo that reflects the client's vision and also sets the framework for future collateral and designs created after the logo.

*Integrate logo design elements into consequent design. Myth's interior design elements were based on the color and design tone first established by the logo.*
CAPSULE

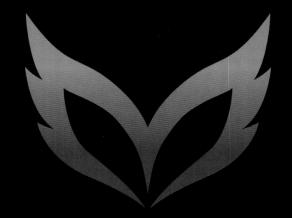

*Strengthen design with observation. To attract multiple audiences, audience, market, and client research guided Myth's logo away from a bias toward any single music genre.*
CAPSULE

# How to Manage Your Research

## AVOID SPLIT ENDS

The research process is like a head of hair. If not maintained, it tangles eventually into a big, snarly mess. If the research process is combed through carefully at the outset, it remains more manageable. There are four steps to achieving this:

1. Temper bias. Bias has a major effect on research outcomes. So give thought to where specific bias originates and then work to offset its influence. Keep in mind that bias exists in any and all research, so completely eliminating it is impossible.

2. Understand a variety of methodologies and what they deliver. Observation is the most authentic methodology, because there is little or no interaction between the observer and subject. This method best identifies specific behaviors.

Surveys are often the most efficient data-gathering method. Historically, these relied heavily on the U.S. Postal Service. Today, the Internet has made this process very convenient. It allows researchers to gather mountains of data from willing participants in the form of either open- or closed-ended questions. Data integrity relies heavily on question wording and the sample used.

Face-to-face interviews are done in one-to-ones, dyads, or triads. There is always one interviewer; the terms refer to the number of interviewees: one, two, or three, respectively. Each combination offers its own unique benefit. However, face-to-face interviews typically offer much of the authenticity of observation, along with the convenience of survey-like feedback.

Focus groups are ideally suited to researchers looking to discover ideas, beliefs, or language around the subject matter. However, focus groups are dangerous when testing ideas or gathering specific data for analysis.

Field studies combine observation and face-to-face interviews done "in the field." They offer authenticity because they probe near consumers' moments of decision. They lend brand research the credibility of authentic context. Field research is often more expensive to conduct, but resulting data is likely more robust and valuable to the creative process. When in doubt, field studies are always a good bet.

3. Use thoughtful sampling. When predicting something specific—say, the outcome of a country's

*Fringe segments are not static. They are defined relative to the perspective of the researcher. The person on the fringe according to one subject area could be considered mainstream according to the parameters of another study.*

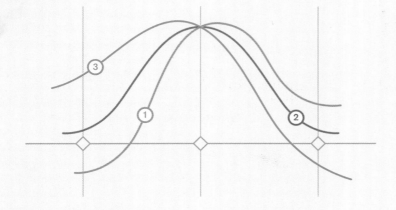

① **POPULATION OF MUSIC LISTENERS**     ② **POPULATION OF MOVIE WATCHERS**     ③ **POPULATION OF PEDAL BIKE RIDERS**

election—a larger percentage of the target market size is required. This percentage is a confident gauge of the prediction. In situations in which researchers seek general knowledge rather than hard numbers, a sample size of ten percent or less of each audience segment should suffice. The key is to have a sample large enough to defend findings confidently.

4. Believe in the bell curve. When conducting research with large sample sizes and situations in which you're predicting future behavior, confidence levels and margins of error are important. In most situations, you will only have to understand that large confidence numbers are good and small are bad. And for margin of error, the opposite is true.

The following eight steps should steer research projects in the correct direction. Once these are covered, move on to the details. And do it quickly, because there are a lot of them. Here is a basic checklist:

1. *Recruit participants*
2. *Write a discussion guide or questionnaire*
3. *Conduct interviews or research*
4. *Transcribe findings*
5. *Analyze results*
6. *Draw out recommendations*
7. *Create the report*
8. *Present it to the client*

Sounds daunting, but rest assured: If you manage the details now, you'll have better research later.

PLANNING | CREATING | IMPLEMENTING

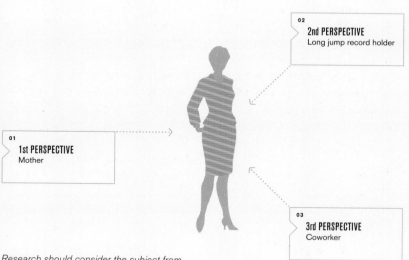

**01**
**1st PERSPECTIVE**
Mother

**02 2nd PERSPECTIVE**
Long jump record holder

**03 3rd PERSPECTIVE**
Coworker

*Research should consider the subject from multiple perspectives. One research method equals one perspective. Three methods equal three perspectives. To her children, this woman is a mother; to judges, she's a strong competitor, etc. No one perspective completely represents the whole woman.*

# How to Test a Logo

## HOUSTON, WE HAVE A HINDENBURG

"Fantastic squirrel!" Encouraging words, if said logo is indeed a squirrel. If it's supposed to be an elephant, you've got a small problem. But not to worry. The planning phase is the time to uncover these issues. It allows you to wrangle them before they charge into the real world and do any major damage.

Testing is a euphemism for disaster management. It uncovers any previously overlooked flubs—because it's surprisingly easy to miss big-picture stuff when working so closely to a project. Before embarking on a project, keep in mind that testing can do great damage when applied at inappropriate stages of the design process. For instance, never, ever, use testing to make a final decision on a logo. You risk nixing a design that is ahead of its time—which would be a pity, since those are often the best designs.

When you've got some work and you're ready to test it, a discussion guide is indispensable. It's a simple document that expedites information gathering by organizing the process. Effective discussion guides include both simple rating questions and plenty of open-ended questions asking how individuals feel about the design. Keep it close—you'll need it.

Then, start scheduling face-to-face interviews. Phone interviews will suffice, in a pinch. Ask questions based on your guide, but also feel free to ad-lib if it feels more appropriate. When you get responses, learn to recognize when and how personal views influence feedback. Sniff out highly emotional language. Once you find it, dig. Participants may say they hate the design. Or overwhelmingly love it. Neither reaction is better or worse than the other. The value is in finding out *why* people feel what they feel. Keep probing until the genesis of

the emotion reveals itself. Consider feedback against that of the entire population. Then determine whether it's specific to the individual or is shared by others.

Research is often counterintuitive, especially at this point. Logically, it follows that the more people who love the logo, the better it is. Right? Isn't it a bad thing when everyone hates it? Not necessarily. Actually, the more emotion involved, the better the chance that someone will remember what he or she is observing. Average gets ignored. Love and hate get people talking, looking, and thinking.

However, it should be noted that, though a logo can work if it is hated, it can't work if it's offensive. Logo testing should filter out any logo components that offend or insult any segments of the audience.

## DOMAINS OF TESTING: BOUNDARIES PROVIDE A SAFE TESTING AREA

Anything can be tested and proven to have bad attributes, given a large enough sample. Focus on the following four domains of testing, to avoid the individual who tests well from damaging every other comment on the logo design.

**Emotional responses:**
The first emotional word an audience associates with the logo. Then, the second.

**Competition:**
How does the logo fit in with, remind them of, or stand out from the competitive set?

**Brand attributes:**
Which brand attributes does it communicate? Which ones does it miss?

**Cultural connotations:**
What cultural messages are being communicated by a logo like this? Of what other images does it remind the audiences?

*The obvious might not be so. Testing reveals that this preliminary concept for the Gear6 logo has a negative visual connection. It's too easy to misconstrue it as offensive, so it's removed from the options.* CAPSULE

THERE ARE TWO SPECIES OF DESIGN BUDGET: WHALES AND SHRIMP. DON'T FRET IF YOU'VE GOT A SHRIMP. THE TRUE DETERMINANT OF SUCCESS IS IN THE TECHNIQUE, NOT THE BAIT. GREAT STRATEGISTS KNOW HOW TO CAPTURE GREAT DESIGN WITHOUT THE AID OF SHINY BELLS AND WHISTLES.

EFFORT,
PLAN, AND
SIMPLE

# Fundamentals of Planning

The beauty is in the process. Planning before pencil meets paper or palm meets mouse is essential to any logo design, small or large. The old adage is true and easy enough to prove: "Fail to plan and you're planning to fail."

Why doesn't everyone plan? Most do but don't plan enough, because it's considered boring. But planning doesn't have to be tedious and long-winded. It just needs to be thorough, mindful, and well thought out. And remember, work done in planning strengthens the brand story, inspires better design, and engages the client in your process. All of these impact the "P" on your P&L. Provide a healthy habitat for your design by spending time understanding four important groups: company, collaborators, competitors, and customers.

# Company

## LAYING THE BRAND ARCHITECTURE'S FOUNDATION

Brand architecture is a loaded term. But what does it mean, really? For the purpose of explanation, imagine a brand as an office building. Brand architecture is the congress of vents, boilers, and copper guts supplying power to the building's occupants day after day, keeping everything running. The logo is the lobby of the building, the gleaming, sleek, leather-bound wrapping. Before fussing over the lobby's light fixtures, worry about the state of the building's wiring. Because all light fixtures look the same in the dark.

A brand's architecture has four basic components: features, benefits, emotional rewards, and archetypes. Features, benefits, and emotional rewards explicitly express brand offerings, outlining exactly what the brand does for individuals. The brand archetype is a metaphor that communicates the same offerings on an abstract level. Rather than *say* what the brand stands for, the archetype *shows* what it stands for.

To understand the difference between the four components, let's dissect the messaging on a tube of toothpaste. *Features* describe the product or brand itself, often in single words such as "minty" and "whitening." *Benefits* are tangible advantages individual consumers enjoy, such as "fresh breath" or "whiter smile." They're mainly rational. *Emotional rewards* are the psychological advantages that consumers take away, such as "confidence" and "attractiveness." These often are not stated explicitly on the packaging but, rather, are implied.

The *archetype* is the personality through which offerings are delivered. All four together comprise the basic framework for the brand architecture.

Brand architecture also contains four supporting elements—key messages, position, promise, and one prominent unmet need—and are meant to supplement and reinforce the four basic components. *Key messages* present the brand in digestible amounts: bite-sized sentences or phrases tailored to a variety of audiences. These audiences can range from members of the media to executive teams and customers. *Position* identifies the brand's place in the minds of consumers and in the competitive battlefield. It's relative to the competitive landscape, competing both for dollars and share of audience attention. The *promise* is what a brand pledges to do for the individual. The promise is at the core of the brand and should manifest itself in anything that communicates something about the brand. Successful brands set realistic, passionate, and valuable promises and then deliver on the promise with each interaction. Language for these three can be inspired by a variety of sources, including in the mission, vision, and values of the organization. With these three, the brand architecture is nearly complete.

The daunting *unmet need* is both a conclusion and a connection. It ties everything else back to the business strategy. So what unmet need does the product, service, experience, or business fulfill? Unmet needs are often hiding out within the pages of business strategies or with the leadership team. To find it, begin by asking, "What does the brand offer that no one else does? What fundamental, currently unmet need does it fulfill?" Enough debate and exploration will clarify the answer. This completes the link between the business strategy and the brand strategy.

PROMISE

BEHAVIORS +
UNMET NEED

ARCHETYPE + POSITION

EMOTIONAL REWARDS

FEATURES + BENEFITS + KEY MESSAGES

*A brand's architecture is designed so all the elements support the brand promise. Study the different building blocks before defining a strong brand.*

*Unmet Need: DrySoda is a sophisticated non-alcoholic drink that seeks to fulfill a perceived gap in the high-end beverage market.* TURNSTYLE

*Archetype: Fox River Socks' newly launched line of "shucking awesome" socks are woven from sustainable corn fiber. The globe logo, illustrated by a tattoo artist, fuses the brand's outlaw archetype with its responsible practices.* CAPSULE

POLYTECH.MONS

*Emotional Reward: Polytech.Mons' logo symbolizes the emotional rewards the institution offers students. These include personal and professional achievement, discovery, and higher knowledge.* EX NIHILO

# Customers

## THE CUSTOMER IS A QUIZZICAL CREATURE

Clients like to know that the designer is educated about the customer. When you can speak authoritatively about target markets and key demographics, it reflects well on your design. This doesn't mean the design needs to be explicitly driven by the client's customer. A logo needs simply to reflect the brand attributes and audience. That said, a little business savvy goes a long way with the suits and ties.

Consumer. Target market. Shopper. Business strategists use many words to describe one thing: the customer. Labeling customers seems important, but understanding them is far more important. This is accomplished by understanding the meaning of basic business language, not memorizing labels such as "soccer mom."

Before conducting any customer research, be sure the methods are valid and agreed upon by the client and a research professional. Solid research will build a strong foundation for the rest of the project.

When decoding customers, context reveals quite a bit. Get context by spending a day as you imagine the customer would. Walk his or her path. See what the customer sees. Feel what the customer feels. Then observe the customer to see how he or she behaves in that same context. Watch how he or she interacts with the brand, decides to buy, use, or even dispose of it. Are there differences? Were any assumptions overturned?

Designers work in a world of Pantone rainbows and rich materials. Research interviewing is a world of checked boxes and dry business language. It may prove less than stimulating for most designers, but it is an important complement to raw observation. To begin, formulate questions aimed at understanding beliefs and test previous observations against what the interviewee says. Take down everything, even if it sounds irrelevant at the time. Once everything has been gathered and there is a more complete picture, take time to filter out what truly is not of use. It's imperative to do this because people can be deceptive and often lie to researchers. They'll tell researchers what they think they want to hear and hide embarrassing opinions. Truthfully, raw observation almost always delivers more valid results than interviews. This is because raw observation studies natural behavior and not formulated response. That being said, face-to-face and one-on-one interviews are still very valuable in that they help prove or put to rest theories drawn from raw observation.

The concept behind Buck 'n' Jims line of spice rubs is a quirky blend of redneck soul and gourmet ingredients. Its unconventional approach gains the attention of Internet trend hunters DailyCandy.com. CAPSULE

Engage customers by integrating an interesting cultural reference. Here the Buck 'n' Jims logo invites conversation; it's the visual equivalent of a witty comment.

## SPREADING MESSAGES, SOWING GROWTH

Starshine Academy is dedicated to "sowing" the world's best community schools where they've never grown before—in at-risk communities around the world. With its roots in a charter school that transforms the lives of kids in one of Arizona's poorest and most dangerous neighborhoods, Starshine wanted to update its identity before starting the second, third, hundredth, or thousandth Starshine Academy. The challenge for Lucid Brands? Create one compelling logo that would convey Starshine's powerful mission and resonate with many different audiences.

As the ultimate "end users," students needed to relate to the logo. Because the school spans K–12, it had to appeal to kids who are just being kids, as well as to kids *having* kids. For parents, the logo can reinforce their trust in the school.

Starshine's founder, Tricia Adams, and its governing and corporate boards were also key audiences. These supporters comprise a "who's who" in architecture, music, technology, social causes, business, education, and other fields. Because of this, it was imperative that the brand strategy and new logo not only meet their high standards but properly express their ideals, as well.

# STARSHINE ACADEMY™

*For Starshine Academy to spread internationally, the logo needed to convey the school's identity to prominent influencers.* LUCID BRANDS

Kids, parents, and the broader community all interact with the logo design. They are the main end users and part of the many pieces of the complex audience with which the logo must resonate.

In addition to speaking with multiple audiences, the identity and logo needed clearly to position Starshine Academy as a world-class organization—ready and worthy of substantial investment. Seeding schools across the globe takes the support of prominent educators, philanthropic leaders, foundations, pundits, social leaders, NGOs, and governments. These influencers are attuned to the quality and meaning of brand symbols, so to reach this audience, Starshine's new logo needed to be crafted with the same attention as that given Fortune 500 companies.

Starshine's message is, "Imagine if you could grow the world's best schools where they've never grown before. Sow them like seeds through the countryside, into cities, and across the planet. At Starshine Academy, that's not just our dream, it's our mission." Once Lucid Brands understood Starshine's unique ability to change children's lives and bring hope to communities, it envisioned a sower of seeds becoming a sower of stars. This sower symbol, seen in the history and art of almost every culture, captured the "Starshine effect." The idea conveyed that the school and its teachers would bring hope to each of their students. Each student would in turn bring hope to others.

Starshine Academy's logo is integrated throughout its teaching materials, from standard teacher's manuals to instructional CDs. The resulting family of educational resources evokes Starshine Academy's personality and purpose.

The symbol allows children to imagine themselves as sowers. Careful consideration ensures that it appears youthful and gender-neutral. By making stars the seeds, the sower image acts as a bridge between the sowing metaphor and Starshine's name. The thirteen stars are symbolic. They represent Starshine's K–12 grades, generations, and stages of knowledge. The new illustration's color carries over from the previous logo. It's a bright, optimistic, and familiar yellow-orange that kids and adults alike associate with bright school buses. The logotype was created to act as a pathway for the sower. A supporting mechanism, the capitalized Trade Gothic Light type provides the sower with a simple, strong patch of ground, capable of fostering growth.

What's next? The new identity is just one part of the effort to spread Starshine Academy. New schools are being planned, and a training center is under development. The effort is in full swing to rally the support needed to bring Starshine Academy to every child who needs it. Starshine Academy's world-class logo helps gain credibility in the eyes of its target audience of potential supporters: sophisticated international organizations.

*"Imagine if you could grow the world's best schools where they've never grown before. Sow them like seeds through the countryside, into cities, and across the planet. At Starshine Academy, that's not just our dream, it's our mission."*

*While researching the idea of a sower, inspired by Starshine's mission, Lucid Brands found this image of folk hero Johnny Appleseed.*

Sower
Might be a boy or a girl

K-12 stars

Positive stride

Logotype acts as a path

# STARSHINE ACADEMY™

Trademark

Lucid Brands collaborated with identity designer Joe Finocchiaro to refine the design and capture the spirit of the sower's stride. The sower figure is gender-neutral and maintains a positive, forward motion. Each of the thirteen stars symbolizes one of Starshine's grade levels, while Starshine Academy's logotype and trademark act as a path for the sower.

# Collaborators

DOES YOUR BRAND HAVE STUFF ON ITS FACE?

If you want a brand to be popular, it needs to look presentable. Logo design is the most obvious example of this. The logo is a brand's haircut. Haircuts are surface treatments, but they speak volumes about the person they top off. Where would Elvis be had he opted for a bland, blond crew cut? If a brand bucks trends, the logo should allude to that. If it's buttoned-down and hard-nosed, the logo should look buttoned-down and hard-nosed. Look the part. Pretty straightforward, no?

Mother was right. It's what's on the inside that counts. Of course, she's the one who was always fussing over your shirts and smoothing your cowlicks. Appearances aren't everything, but they aren't nothing, either. How you look is an external reflection of internal values. When a disheveled logo squats in the corner of an advertisement or sprawls out lazily on a piece of signage, it's sure to turn off a lot of people from the get-go.

Brands are a lot like people. They have personalities, names, and values. They even have friends. Except that, in the land of brands, a "friend" is called a "collaborator." And these collaborators come in many forms: competitors, customers, media, and industry organizations, among others. Basically, they're anyone or anything that can promote your brand and advance its reputation without getting compensated with cash. They talk to friends, who talk to friends. And they talk to friends. Word-of-mouth connection is one of the oldest methods of building a strong brand. It's also the best heeded, because it's an authentic form of communication.

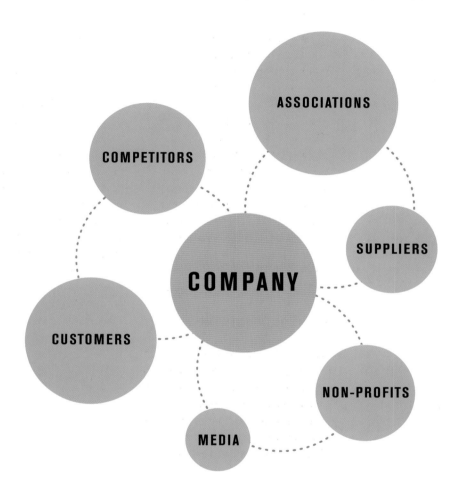

*Collaborators often pop up in unexpected places. Brainstorm a bit about where you lack knowledge and look for people in those areas who can help fill in the gaps.*

# Competitors

## BEATING THE BRAND

See it out of the corner of your eye? Feel the hairs on your neck stand up? That's them. The competition. Why, at this very moment, they're undoubtedly hatching a plan to sneak away a piece of your client's market pie. If you want to beat them, heed that old saying: "Keep friends close; keep your enemies closer." Good advice. But before you invite them over, you should know their names: primary, secondary, and tertiary.

Primary competitors have brand values that overlap yours in a significant way. This is the result of one of two things: either your brand messaging is generic, or it's so good, competitors copy it. Whatever the case, it's important to stay unique. Often, products in a category have similar features and benefits. A distinct brand gives you the upper hand by highlighting a feature or benefit that's unique to your service or product. If it's done well, the brand will go a long way in selling your offering over that of a direct competitor.

Primary competitors butt heads on an hourly, daily, and weekly basis. Understanding primary competitors helps define day-to-day tactics. However, successful long-term strategies look beyond current primary competitors. Long-term design strategy should focus on voyaging to places where there are no primary competitors. The final goal is for the client to compete only with secondary and tertiary competitors.

Secondary competitors include all those above, below, or just outside your client's competitive circle. The brands offer a realistic alternative to your client but aren't competing directly. Secondary competitors appear periodically on the competitive landscape but never offer a consistent threat. But, they do require consideration. If they are successful, they may quickly grow into primary competitors. Additionally, because they offer an alternative, changes in marketplace dynamics, economic conditions, or other uncontrollable factors could change how secondary competitors compete with your client's brand.

Tertiary competitors are like newborn siblings. Technically, they don't compete directly for quantifiable things, such as food and shelter. But they do take away attention that would otherwise go to your client. Tertiary competitors compete for an audience's attention by offering similar distribution or communication channels. They can't always take market share, but they can take mindshare. So they require some attention. For instance, your client may not compete directly with everyone advertising in a particular magazine, but when an advertisement appears in that context, the client does compete for attention.

Other tertiary competitors include the pocket of potentials, those who are not competing directly but have the potential or desire to do so in the future. This group can offer both threats and interesting opportunities. Understand them and know their ability to innovate or acquire. Also, learn a bit about the future of your category. Then make a judgment as to whether these competitors are friends or foes.

# COMPETITIVE LANDSCAPING EXERCISE

··· Start gathering artifacts. All communication elements are eligible, from business cards and invoices to signage, advertisements, and vehicles. The more you dig up, the clearer the picture will become.

··· Place everything on a wall, organized first by communication device and then by competitor. Initially, this might feel like a visual audit. But it will soon turn into much more.

··· Invite designers, writers, and objective businesspeople to spend time with the wall. Give the writers a particular flag color. Give the designers another, and so on. Post-it notes are handy for this.

··· Ask each person to identify and mark similarities and differences in both the language and visual presentations of each brand. Have participants look at everything, from size of the business card to type, images, and common colors. The color-coded flags will form patterns where the commonalities exist from the perspective of each group. Have each group articulate the similarities found.

··· Photograph the results. Then articulate the findings by similarity and by communication device.

··· Now flip the exercise. Have the participants identify significant differences. This part of the exercise will likely reveal the leaders in the category—or, at the very least, those most capable of thinking and acting differently, the way leaders often do.

## THE GEAR6 BRAND: HOW DO YOU MAKE INNOVATION STAND OUT?

The word "innovation" suffers from the same problem as do the words "strategy" and "creative." Like so many linguistic laser pointers, the business community has overused them to the point where they've lost their original brilliance.

The Gear6 name and identity support one another. Its logo offers a hidden message found on a keyboard. Just hit the shift key + the number six. Green sets Gear6 apart from a sea of blue technology logos. CAPSULE

In a world where the word innovative is anything but, how do you communicate the genuine article without sounding insincere? Well, it seems the best way to appear innovative is to act innovative. The logo is the perfect tool for this end. Gear6's logo matches its technology products in terms of innovation and design excellence. And it communicates this in the most convincing manner—through silent, visible reality.

Silicon Valley is a tough place in which to stand out as innovative. Gear6 knows. It keeps offices in Menlo Park, California—possibly the most competitive stretch of land in the world for technology brands. The technology hardware systems category has plenty of large competitors, including EMC, IBM, Intel, NEC, HP, and Sun Microsystems. However, Gear6 found an area in Silicon Valley in which it could lead in innovation—its logo design.

![IBM logo](IBM logo in white horizontal stripes on grey background) ®

*Industries start to form patterns and behaviors based on historical leaders in the industry. Fit in or stand out—but before doing either one, know how your logo's look and feel gels with the business strategy.*

PAUL RAND

Blue happens to be the most inoffensive color globally, but it is also the most common technology brand color. It doesn't work hard to set one brand apart from the competitive set.

# CREATI

**IG**

THE CREATION OF ART IS NOT THE
FULFILLMENT OF A NEED BUT THE CREATION
OF A NEED. THE WORLD NEVER NEEDED
BEETHOVEN'S FIFTH SYMPHONY UNTIL
HE CREATED IT. NOW WE COULD NOT LIVE
WITHOUT IT.  – LOUIS I. KAHN

# MILK COMES WITH A DEFINITE EXPIRATION DATE. LOGOS DO NOT. WHEN YOU SELL A BRAND OWNER A FRESH LOGO, MAKE SURE THAT PERSON KNOWS HOW TO STORE IT PROPERLY. OR IT MAY SOUR PREMATURELY.

# Essential Criteria

Set standards for your logo design work. Beyond that, know your client's and your creative community's standards. Your work will be more grounded, and you'll project confidence in the design philosophy to the client. Standards are necessary, reaffirming, and reassuring. It's not so much what the specific standards are but simply their existence and consistent presence that is important.

There are three main design criteria by which to build standards: simplicity, uniqueness, and metaphoric symbolism. *Simplicity* equals strength. The less convoluted and the more direct a concept, the more memorable and effective it is. *Uniqueness* establishes visual separation—helpful when your brand is vying for attention in a crowded marketplace. Use of *metaphor* is a core element of brand storytelling. The stronger the metaphor, the stronger the story. And the stronger the story, the more memorable the logo.

In the end, all the standards you set will take aim at memorability. Simple is memorable, metaphors are essentially memory aids, and uniqueness is noticeable and then memorable. The higher and more resolute your standards for these three, the more the audience should remember your client's brand.

# Criteria 1: Simplicity

## EINSTEIN WAS A MAJOR SIMPLETON

"Everything should be made as simple as possible but not simpler," Albert Einstein said. And he should know. His theory of relativity manages to summarize all existing matter into five simple characters.

Simplification is pivotal to logo design. Consider Google. It is building an empire on a simplified search process, and its logo reflects this strategy. Because the logo is so simple, it can be accessorized with everything from holiday ornaments to specific business sectors. The more simple, the more intuitive, the more approachable. Simply stated, simplicity is a force multiplier.

Simplicity is essential for many reasons, the most important being society's current volume of messages. Consumers are bombarded with more and more information every day. Because of this, designers of all disciplines must simplify their messages so they can be absorbed before another one shoves them aside. Logos marking almost every piece of any given organization's communications or products constitute a large percentage of this visual chaos. It is essential that designers reduce a logo design's elements down to only its most essential components.

Refinement is the act of simplifying or paring down. After a client accepts a design, some may consider the work completed. But, this is the moment when another round of refinement is often required. It is best to leave it and return later with fresh eyes, because the chances of discovering unseen redundancies increase. Diligence is rewarded with uncluttered communication and clear end products.

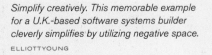

Simplify creatively. This memorable example for a U.K.-based software systems builder cleverly simplifies by utilizing negative space.
ELLIOTTYOUNG

**PocketCard**

Convey dimension with simple structure. This logo represents a prepaid card system and elegantly achieves visual dimension.
SEGURA, INC.

Simplify without losing personality. This logo for a U.K.–based paint-your-own pottery retailer conveys a personal, craft-inspired feel through simple, unique, visual gestures.
WOLFF OLINS

# RED WINGS

*Simplify multiple metaphors into one identity. The logo for Red Wing Shoes' casual line conveys both a shield and wing in three simple pieces.* CAPSULE

# Criteria 2: Uniqueness
## REBEL WITH A CAUSE

For some, school was a party in a box, neatly prepackaged with autumn football games and wrist corsages. For others, high school was as uninspiring as cafeteria food. Many of these "others" eventually grew up to be creative professionals, a role in which uniqueness is in the job description and clients applaud creativity.

Uniqueness serves clients in two major ways. Legally, it ensures that clients remain safe from litigation. Creatively, it enriches the client's brand and makes it more memorable. But there's a difference between being truly unique and just being different. Genuine uniqueness stands out from the crowd and provokes further thought. It is different for the sake of something better and permeates its host at all levels.

Being different, though, doesn't inherently denote substance. Many things and people are different just for the sake of being different. It's an aesthetic surface treatment that doesn't push forward so much as shuffle in another direction, for better or worse. Don't confuse the two. If there's no substance, the audience won't have anything to attach to, and the brand message will glop off sadly, like a mashed mound from an upturned lunch tray.

If you seek unique design answers in client meetings, you may find yourself right back in school again. Your new ideas may be treated like new kids, attracting snickers, jeers, and rolling eyes. Don't fold. You are now paid to think differently and to help your client see the brand's creative potential. Fight the little voices of doubt in your head. Fight the loud voices of clients on the conference phone. Fight kindly, gently, and rationally, but fight nonetheless. It's your job to push boundaries. If you make your case and the client still isn't buying, then you've done what you can. Only then should you begin open negotiations.

*A fish by any other stroke would not be as unique. The raw brush stroke creates a simple and unique Kanji-inspired logo for the Osaka Sushi Bar. Just any old fish would not pass the test.* CDI STUDIOS

*Photographer Frank Nesslage uses his nickname, Nessi, to inspire his logo. Professionally attaching to Loch Ness is definitely a unique approach. It's also clever, interesting, and hard to forget.* DZIALIFORNIA

*Manufactured stories are for kids. The Children's Museum of Utah, USA, has a programming activity and exhibition group called Story Factory. The logo for Story Factory is a unique, playful visual.*
CC GRAPHIC DESIGN

A distinct look in the financial services category requires exploration beyond traditional comfort zones. The Einfach Investieren by Fidelity Germany is a great example of uniqueness in a category. LIGALUX

# Criteria 3: Metaphor

## ALL THE WORLD'S A LOGO

PLANNING | CREATING | IMPLEMENTING

Metaphors make great stories. Ask any writer. Better yet, read a book. Metaphors encode experiences and artifacts into base denominators, so that everyone who shares stock with the common denominator can feel them.

Metaphors target the core of the human psyche by tapping into cultural heritage. Using symbolism and archetypes, they sear memories into the mind. Strong metaphors are essential to the brand story. Worthwhile metaphors extend to logo design. Ideation logically starts with metaphor exploration, and the first step is the briefing.

The challenge of any organization or business is to communicate who it is and what it stands for and to accomplish this for an audience that is often more interested in a nagging hangnail or when it has to pick up the kids.

Any brand's surest bet is to identify itself simply, engagingly, and directly. When this is the case, don't worry about relaying all the intricate details. Rather, ensure that your story is consistent.

We all know of Enron, Goldman Sachs, and Microsoft. Do we know all the finer points of their business? No. Who would want to? The point is not to make consumers completely understand the brand; it's more important to make them trust the brand.

One example of this is the logo for Cerenity senior care facilities based in Minnesota, USA. The logo communicates brand values in a direct way that creates a connection for its audience. The butterfly represents growth, beauty, and flight, among many other things. The interior cross is a highly evocative symbol that makes an explicit connection back to the brand's

Christian roots. Together, the butterfly and cross represent the most important values of the senior care facilities.

The story starts with a simile: "The organization is like a butterfly floating over a field of prairie grass—peaceful and tranquil." Then, it should move to a more subtle approach, which is where the metaphor comes into play. "The tranquility of a floating butterfly" is the phrase that inspires the senior care facility's logo design.

A worthwhile story does not change with time, new management, or external rotation. Great metaphors communicate complex stories to a large, diverse audience. Find the right metaphor and you've struck brand gold. It will be the foundation for everything that follows.

**ISLAND QUEEN CRUISE**

*Canada's largest sightseeing cruise ship's logo helps tell its story. The metaphor is a queen's crown floating over the flowing Canadian waters, symbolizing luxury, national pride, and elegance.* RIORDAN DESIGN

*Cerenity's logo design alludes subtly to the organization's Christian faith through metaphor, whereas the name does not.* CAPSULE

*Negative metaphors can be spun positively. Playful naughtiness comes across simply and directly in the Gluttony logo design.* OCTAVO

During the briefing, establish the brand values. This is made up of the brand promise, archetypes, attributes, personality, and other brand fundamentals. Brand values serve as the foundation for consequent metaphor development and should be used as a barometer throughout the process.

*This organization has a dual mission to protect nature and motivate others to participate. The bird and hand are two metaphors that give life to its nonliteral name, Natagora.* EX NIHILO

WANT A HAPPY, HEALTHY BUNDLE OF CREATIVITY? THEN BOTTLE-FEED IT A STEADY DIET OF INFORMATION. SWADDLE IT IN ENTHUSIASM FOR THE MATERIAL OR SUBJECT MATTER. BURP IT REGULARLY, PURGING SUB-PAR IDEAS AS THEY GURGLE. THIS IS HOW YOU CARE FOR CREATIVITY. THIS IS YOUR CREATIVE PROCESS.

DON'T THROW
INSPIRATION OUT
WITH THE BATH WATER.

# Creativity and Knowledge

Your creative process is your special sauce, trump card, and trade secret all rolled into one. Teach employees how to care for it; you'll need help raising it. But that's it. Don't reveal your creative process to outsiders. Especially clients. If the method works, they'll see the results soon enough in their bottom line.

"Creative process" sounds a bit like an oxymoron—like jumbo shrimp or black light. It's like Jackson Pollock splattering by numbers. However, oxymoron it's not. "Process" is a logical part of creativity. For all his random gesturing, Mr. Pollock had a process. He worked on white canvases with four square corners. He picked particular colors and brushed with certain brushes. And most of all, though his splatters seem random when taken individually, together, his works coalesce into a definitive pattern and style.

# Inspiration Sources

## DON'T BE LIKE A FISH OUT OF IDEAS

Give a man a fish and you've fed him, for today. Teach a man to fish and you've fed him for a lifetime. Or at least until he gets sick of seafood. Fishing for ideas is an art form. Seasoned art directors know which bait nabs which prey. They know ideal times and the special, secret "spots" that greenhorns blindly trample past. And when they sense a real tug, they reel in their tethers with nimble, deft pacing. Catching ideas takes time, dedication, and patience.

If you're looking for a place to catch some largemouth ideas, cast your line in a good book. Words of all sizes and shapes zip and nibble at your mind, tugging it into the author's fluid world. Wade through connotations, splash around in symbolism, and ideas will float to the surface faster.

Awards annuals are fine if you're looking to do what has already been done. For something fresh and new that could end up in *next* year's award annual, find quirky, off-the-beaten-path publications. Or publications that are not traditionally associated with the category for which you are designing. For example, your design for a technology firm could be found while flipping through an old French cookbook—or a world atlas. A word, illustration, or recipe could trigger a metaphor or visual language that can be applied to anything, so long as you connect it well.

Beyond books, immerse yourself in the world around you. The most obvious place to go is where the logo design will eventually live: trade shows, retail stores, or along park trails. To find further inspiration, roam to vibrant locales in which culture coagulates, such as community celebrations, plays, and festivals. Also visit destinations where people seek solace and reconnect with themselves.

Creative inspiration also congregates heavily around your contemporaries. Find peers with whom you can bounce ideas, flesh out concepts, and find encouragement. Hardworking freelancers often need to spend time in a design office with other people doing similar work.

The places and activities in which you likely will *not* find creative inspiration are just as common. Watching television is one of these activities.

Children's brain activity has been shown to list off to nil in front of the boob tube. Avoid places in which you are not only alone but also have no external stimulation. On the flip side, avoid overstimulation; the human brain can handle only a certain amount before it emits a tired shudder and its eyes flicker shut.

Don't give up on finding that perfect creative fishing hole. Once you're there, you'll know. When it happens, look around and sketch a map so you can find your way back.

Before you pick up a sketch pad, review the previous work done during the planning stage. Initial work is often a fertile source of inspiration and ideas.

Seek objects with literal and aesthetic value. The inspiration for the logo of this design house, Root Idea, comes from nature. Branches represent design's two spheres of necessity: logic and aesthetics. The hand symbolizes growing ideas. ROOT IDEA

Immerse yourself in another world. While designing the logo for the children's clothing retailer Goodnight Moon, the designer spent time reading children's books and hanging around kids and in the retailer's environment. CAPSULE

Pick simple ideas. The shape and color of grapes growing in rows play into a visually memorable logo design for Mornington Estates Winery. OCTAVO

## IDEATION EXERCISES

One popular metaphor exploration process is called visual ideation, which includes searching magazines, newspapers, websites, video podcasts, and blogs for inspiration. While searching, pick and pull inspirational, relevant images. Once a solid collection has been gathered, hold a team ideation session. Present all the information together and share thoughts. Consider why certain images were intriguing and how this visual charisma can be translated into the project.

A single exercise can run ten minutes; several over a week can add up to multiple hours. There is no need to be overly controlling at this point, but it is important to prepare for a certain level of chaos, because random, unstructured, non-linear thinking is a fundamental component of creative thinking. The only way to find something new is to upset convention. By applying the right amount of focused pressure and conflict, ideas start flowing at an amazing pace. If the initial session does not seem to yield the results you are looking for, remember that patterns can be found later upon closer observation, and when a session is sluggish, move the team on to something completely unrelated.

Don't fall in love with a direction at this stage. Step back and develop several ideas. You may have something genuinely insightful. If you get too attached to one idea, you're shutting out other possibilities and turning off the creative faucet.

Another simple exercise requires one marker, five pages of large paper, and at least three to five functioning brains (or six to ten halfwits, if that's all you can find). More than fifteen will invite chaos and muffle less outspoken members. Ideation sessions should always be somewhat intimate affairs conducted with an abbreviated set of core, creative minds in the room. During these exercises, challenge the group to come up with twenty ideas in twenty minutes. These do not have to be solid, well-formed ideas; members should open their minds and not feel uncomfortable about suggesting seemingly silly things, because these often ignite more legitimate concepts.

## METAPHORS: CREATING IDEAS IN A BOX

Identifying metaphors needn't be a random process. Just remember, the structure should focus on ideas, not the process. Try not to overly refine one idea. As an idea develops, have the discipline to put it aside once it has enough structure for someone to get it. Moving on quickly is essential to success.

## THE VISUAL METAPHOR MATRIX EXERCISE

1. Gather all relevant materials. Use them to reconnect to the client's brand, promise, and personality.

2. Identify the top five attributes of the client's brand. Examples: speed, simplicity, performance, care, community, love.

3. Identify five basic words that are simple enough for a child to understand. Examples: person, tree, house, nature, animal, word, flight. Start broad. These words can be narrowed and refined into more descriptive terms later.

4. Create a matrix by placing the brand attributes on one axis and the visually descriptive, broad words on the other.

5. Fill in the boxes with ideas, sketches, or whatever comes to mind. These "images" are the interface between a particular brand attribute and a basic word. Images will suggest further words, and words will suggest further images.

6. Keep the machine on spin cycle. From this process, many combinations will pour out. Unrelated elements will reveal unexpected and creative metaphors.

| VISUAL DESCRIPTIVE WORDS >> | | | | | | |
|---|---|---|---|---|---|---|
| **BRAND ATTRIBUTES >>** | People | Nature | Houses | Tools | Animals | Science |
| Speed | | | | | | |
| Simplicity | | | | | | |
| Performance | | | | | | |
| Care | | | | | | |
| Community | | | | | | |
| Love | | | | | | |

*Create boxes and boxes of metaphors. Having places to put ideas helps push the design concepts onto the page.*

# Surrounding Layout

## ARE YOU BUILDING AN ANCHOR OR A SAIL?

Not long ago, plump ships glided into the ports of majestic empires, straining under vast cargoes of spices, textiles, and adventures plucked from faraway colonies. Today, logos act like mighty vessels, transporting brand messages wherever the brand roams, from shopping carts and refrigerators to the opposite ends of the Earth.

Effective logos are like ships, but bad logos act more like anchors, fixing brands tightly to one moment in time and leaving little room for the brand to move. They are often missing one of three principal elements: simplicity, metaphor, and uniqueness. Consider how your designs embody each of these, in what capacity and in what applications. Also consider and visualize how the design fits into both the three-dimensional and the two-dimensional world. Today's technology makes this a fairly easy process. Show

clients logos in their surrounding layouts. For presentations, paste the logo onto signage, stationery systems, and packaging. It's easy to get excited about a logo when it's on your computer screen. Shortcomings spring up in real-world applications.

The logo design's surrounding layout takes many forms. It's not the logo designer's responsibility to make sure all future communications are up to snuff. But if standards are high, you can inspire your client to achieve them.

A logo on its own won't transform a good company into a bad one. But it can make a good company *look* bad. The logo should be an asset, not a liability. A good logo is one that contributes to brand success. The best you can strive for is to design a logo that exemplifies the brand and tells a story in the simplest form

possible. Also, design the logo to reflect where the brand is going, not just where it's been.

You'll know when you've designed an anchor of a logo, one that's stale and heavy. You'll know because you'll encounter it in a trade publication, shrunken and tucked into an inconspicuous corner of a much better-designed advertisement. The small logo will sink under the rest of the brand, hidden from view. That is, until the client finally completely cuts ties with it and hoists a new logo high into the light of day. The surrounding layout impacts a logo design if the logo designer considers it. Consider it and your design will have a better chance of survival.

*Become part of the environment. The Union logo design is an integral part of the surrounding layout. It contributes to the rest of the design, making it more memorable.* CRUSH

*Envision logos in three-dimensional surroundings. The Fashion Center's logo design goes beyond a two-dimensional symbol, solidifying into a three-dimensional brand object.* PENTAGRAM

# Color and Clients

PUT YOUR PANTONES ON ONE LEG AT A TIME

One of the most important things to know about color is how to make a client think about it rationally. A lot of clients burden colors with emotional associations. For no reason in particular, one man's burnt sienna is another man's nightmare. When discussing color with clients, let your swatches do the talking.

Once your swatches have spoken their piece, then you can exercise your lips. Ask what the client likes, what the client's audience would like, what will make the logo design distinct in the existing market. Make sure clients factor in how the logo's color will extend into every area of business, from overall system color to office carpeting.

Let your client pick a few favorites. Then review how each will work with the brand objectives, based on competitors, industry, and brand personality. Tell the client in what ways the color gets people talking and buying into the brand. Remember, the rainbow is infinite. Focus the client, or you may never find the end of it.

If your client wants to build an innovative brand, guide the color accordingly. Drop names of important brands that have dared to color where no one has colored before. Cemstone is a great example. The Midwest construction cement company owns robin's egg blue. However, that specific shade is also internationally associated with Tiffany's jewelry house, a brand perched a million debutantes away from construction's rugged terrain. That's precisely why Cemstone's adoption of blue is so brilliant. The vibrant hue busts the brand free from the comfortable gray fog in which industry competitors quietly drift off.

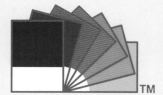  

*Sometimes color is the brand. One of the world's top brands, Pantone, defines the meaning and standard of color. Its logo is flexible and clear.* PENTAGRAM

Think also about what colors have the potential to communicate a negative attribute. Understand the impact and stigmas of specific color, so when your client brings in a swatch of electric grape juice purple, you can deftly quell the situation.

Probably the most common mistake in logo design is creating a logo that requires more than one color to retain the original concept. A successful logo needs the ability to present the same concept in one color as it does in three. If the logo requires three colors, your client will find it necessary always to use more than two colors; in some media, that can be costly relative to the value they will see.

Once a primary color has been chosen, the next big step is finding a secondary color and the rest of the palette. The second color should obviously complement the primary and should also work with any other color in the palette. The color is not what should distinguish the logo in the marketplace.

vocal
consulting group

10:2:6

vocal revolution

private voice client

*What does color say? The Vocal brand's logo comprises overlapping complementary colors, a design that works for a variety of groups within the organization.* ELEMENT

*Deconstruct color. A color's context matters and has a tremendous impact on the final result. In the jewelry category, Tiffany's classic blue sets the industry standard. It is registered under its founding date, 1837. In the construction category, Cemstone's robin's egg blue is a non-traditional color that grabs attention and stands out from traditional construction yellow.* CEMSTONE

# Color and Emotion

## WHAT'S HIDING BEHIND YOUR SHADES

Many things can occur in the blink of your eye. When you look at something, you don't just automatically see it—although that's how it feels. The brain interprets images in stages. First the brain identifies shape, then color. Look at a banana, and you first see the oblong curve and the tapered ends. The shape helps you decide what the image is. Then you see the color. The color helps you decide how you feel about the image. A banana's yellow perks you up. Blueberries soothe. Red fire trucks spark aggression.

Color's influence runs so deeply into the subconscious that we have yet to map out all its wandering tributaries. But the things we do know have led us to respect color's practical purposes. Color can give clear direction when language fails to translate. It's a simple communication device that directs global traffic, helps establish status for everything from the Olympic Games to pie baking contests, and makes organizations stand out. Owning a color is one of

the higher achievements a brand can reach. In 1916, the Merchants Parcel Delivery, a young Seattle operation, adopted brown as its trademark color. Today, the firm still uses brown, but its name is now UPS.

The way to own a color is to choose one that no competitors in your category own. If there are a lot of established, visible brands in your category, this is tricky. Then again, don't get too worried. After all, the color spectrum is infinite. Step outside and identify typical colors. Then let your eyes rest on the atypical ones. Seek options that fit your brand and filter through them, to make sure there isn't a reason certain colors haven't been used before. Take the ones that make it through that filter and consider how well each will work across a variety of media. Considering all the media that exist now, and all that will exist in the near future, this is no small task. Don't worry if your color isn't comfortable at first. In fact, if it is, it may not be different enough from the rest of the existing category.

## COLOR CONSIDERATION PROCESS

Find a color you can own in your category. It will aid brand recognition tremendously and add to brand equity.

Understand color's cultural connotations. Cultural meaning varies greatly. Weed out variations and any negative associations.

Identify a color that consistently communicates from chip to ink, toner, the Web, threads, signage, and standard paint.

Understand how electronic file formats affect color in the files. An .eps file won't treat color in the same way as a .jpg file made for the Web.

Color science is ever-evolving, due to new perspectives and discoveries about how the human brain reacts to colors.

Color impacts memory and contributes meaning to a brand. Proceed with thoughtful discretion and respect for its power.

GE Market Name
Solution Platform

# unsteel

*imagination at work*

GE Consumer & Industrial

crisper

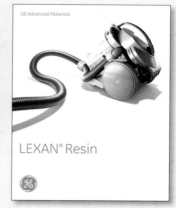

GE Advanced Materials

LEXAN® Resin

GE Healthcare

## uncut
our capabilities

GE Transportation
Aviation

# power

Lorem ipsum dolor sit amet, consectetuer adipiscing elit. Sed orci sapien, rutrum eget, hendrerit non, blandit et, massa. Pellen tesque tempor metus sed purus. Quisque id mauris et urna hendrerit molestie. Cum sociis natoque penatibus et magnis dis parturient montes, nascetur ridiculus mus.

Visit www.ge.com for more details.

*imagination at work*

GE Advanced Materials

2005 product guide

GE Consumer & Industrial
Lighting

## DOUBLE BIAX
## SPECIFICATIONS

Nominal Lamp Dimensions – Inches (mm)

T4 Diameter 1/2" (13mm) - BiaxTM D/E, Single End G24q -1-2-3 4 Pin Base Without Internal Starter

GE Money
Loans

Lorem ipsum dolor sit amet, consectetuer adipiscing elit sed diam nonummy nibh euismod tincidunt ut laoreet dolore magna aliquam erat volut diam nona. Ut wisi enim ad minim veniam, quis nostrud exerci tation ullam.

# 6.6%=

*imagination at work*

no luce, no calore,
no elettricita',
ancora congelato.

GE imagination at work

3500 SERIE

Set a variety of tones. General Electric uses color to convey the varied businesses and perspectives it offers to the global economy.
WOLFF OLINS

# Memory and Meaning

## TIE A STRING AROUND THEIR BRAINS

Long-term memory likes to keep a tidy cerebral cortex. Somewhere at this moment, it's rolling up its sleeves and tossing out the name of that B-list movie star. It probably figures you'll never need it again. Tomorrow, it just may tackle those high school fight song lyrics gathering dust in your medulla oblongata. When it comes to cleaning house, memory is fickle. If you want your logo to stay in people's memories, make it something that attaches to something in people's lives, something they want to remember and maybe even share with friends.

Essentially, make it mean something. Even if the client's line of business is completely uninspiring, find the meaning behind the service or product. Meaning manifests everywhere. Look around you. Think like Andy Warhol. He made soup cans arresting and provocative. Everything has potential. Know the brand, know the audience, and use the logo to connect the two.

Connect the audience and the brand through the brand story, but don't necessarily give it all away. A nice way to make people remember is to pitch out an unfinished sentence. Make them seek a resolution. Make them wonder why the logo for a computer company is a piece of fruit. People will try to make the connection, and when they do, it will have a good chance of sticking with them.

*Smile! The treat for kids is sweet. The treat for parents is the smile the treats inspire. The Joy Co. logo creates a lasting impression with abstracted human faces.* PENTAGRAM

*The American Institute of Architects Fund Campaign for Open Our Doors borrows from a memorable icon, integrating the cityscape in an engaging way.* PENTAGRAM

Wine from a hive, fancy that. WineHaven Winery and Vineyard is a family-run company with a unique history rooted in honey production. The bee logo is a simple mnemonic device that references the WineHaven story. CAPSULE

# Typography

## ALL EYES ARE ON YOUR FACE

Down on the floor. Up on the billboard. Type is crawling around everywhere. And most people don't even know it. Most consumers aren't able, even with some time and a lot of magnification, to tell the difference between Goudy and Garamond, or to begin to care about the implications of using Meta instead of Trade Gothic. Despite this, type can have as much influence as color when put in a designer's hands. To a designer, the difference between Goudy and Garamond is the difference between burlap and tin foil.

The number of typefaces currently available is hard to fathom. Think truckloads of telephone books. The major downside of this typeface overpopulation is that misused typefaces abound. Quite unfortunate, considering that type has a major presence and a subtle but potent ability to convey tone and personality. Consequently, an unreadable or inappropriate typeface has just as much potential to distract from a beautiful logo design as it does to enhance it.

Consider the subtle influences of type and spend time educating your clients. If you can defend the way in which a certain typeface reinforces a core brand message, your clients will value it well into the future.

PLANNING | CREATING | IMPLEMENTING

### HOW TO FIND A TYPE FOR YOUR LOGO DESIGN

▸ 1. Gather the largest library of available typefaces that you can access.

▸ 2. Consider what the brand needs to communicate and identify the brand's fundamental attributes.

▸ 3. Browse typefaces and select a few that communicate some of the brand's attributes.

▸ 4. Conduct type studies by examining how the type works with the letterforms of the brand name.

▸ 5. Consider creating a custom typeface or adapting a particular typeface to make it unique to the client.

▸ 6. Find complementary typefaces that work as a secondary typeface with the primary one.

▸ 7. Review the typeface with other designers and ask whether it is communicating what you had intended.

▸ 8. Integrate typefaces into the logo concepts so you can show them in the first presentation to the client.

*Turn convention on its head. The Change logo design uses an ambigram to create a memorable moment of discovery when you happen to see the logo upside down.* SUBPLOT DESIGN INC.

*The simple type solution for the Dutch Presidency of the European Union in 2004 balances three colors and seven unique shapes. The elegant, calligraphic logotype creates a logo design that lives in a box, yet thinks outside of it.* STUDIO DUMBAR

*Take a little off the top. The logo type for Yosho evokes clever simplicity with an arresting visual edit. The cropped numerals refer to the Internet marketing company's number based solutions.* SEGURA, INC.

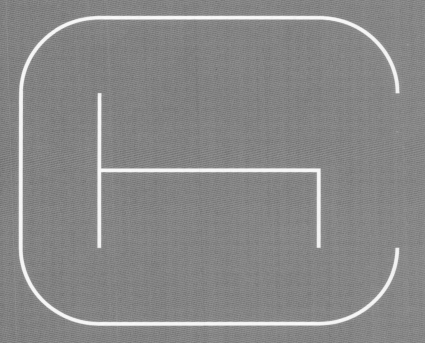

*Shape meaning with typography. The elegant use of type in the CH monogram for Chambers Hotel is a striking example of typography and shape cooperating seamlessly.* PENTAGRAM

# Hierarchy

## LOOK BEFORE YOU CROSS THE UMBRELLA

Umbrella brands protect sub-brands from harsh market elements, casting long shadows of influence across them. In the brand hierarchy, they are the big kahunas. Sub-brands answer to them. If you're working on adding a new sub-brand to an established hierarchy, be careful where you tread. There is most likely a set way of doing things. It won't sit well with the other sub-brands or the umbrella brand if you don't consider how your new logo will get along with their logos.

Gather the umbrella brand and all its sub-brands on the couch for a heart-to-heart. Find out each of the sub-brands' express roles. Who's the leader? Who's the one with the good connections? Who's the rookie? Once you know everyone's place, you'll see the place your sub-brand, and consequently your logo, should occupy. Study how the sub-brands' personalities and roles are reflected in logos. The better you understand all the connected brands when you're designing, the easier it is for the audience to associate the new logo to the umbrella brand.

One sub-brand's logo may lead on the website, in brochures, and business cards. Another, however, may lead in other areas. Each logo has a unique strength, something it can say better than any of the others. In given situations, different ones jump to the front. Let the right brand lead when it should.

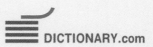

DICTIONARY.com

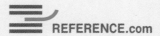

REFERENCE.com

THESAURUS.com

*Hierarchy organizes. Structure and hierarchy are not new words to Lexico. Its sub-brands' logos live alone and also connect straight back to the source.* SEGURA, INC.

# City of Amsterdam

*Within the chaos of a metropolitan area, logo design is implemented with great detail and attention to hierarchy. The St. Andrews' crosses come directly from the city coat of arms, harkening back to the city's heritage.*

EDEN DESIGN

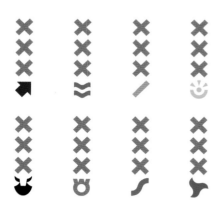

*Three X's mark the spot. Amsterdam's brand comprises a variety of sub-brands under a larger umbrella brand. Each area of the city government has its own sub-brand. The design is ideal for a network organization, such as city government.*

# Protectable

## IMITATION IS THE SINCEREST FORM OF THIEVERY

During the California gold rush, wagonloads of minors clamored to the Pacific Coast armed with homemade tin pan sifters and 24-karat dreams. These days, wealth no longer glitters from the shallow banks of sandy streams. Modern prospectors pan for wealth in the streams of their consciousness. Technology and service industries rely almost completely on ideas.

It's easy to overlook the legal side of the logo design process. Most designers don't consider legalese their forte or their responsibility. But it is—at least, to a point. You can determine this when you sit down with the client and explicitly talk through who is in charge of legal considerations. They may be completely new to the process, so walk them through what needs to be done. Talk to them about

preliminary trademark searches and decide who will contact and hire a lawyer to do the final, comprehensive trademark search. You should always take it upon yourself to search out redundancies with logos in your client's industry category. The Internet makes this a fairly simple process. But after your client decides on a final logo, a legally sound search will require a trained lawyer. Forgo a legal search, and two things can happen. One, your client gets sued by a competitor because the logo you designed looks too similar. Or two, your client's beautiful new logo gets ripped off because it isn't legally protected.

It's also important to remember that just because the client's brand name is trademarked doesn't mean the logo is as well. Competitors can use a different name and a very similar mark.

The rights of first use do offer some protection, but they often don't go far enough to protect your design in a global marketplace. This is important, because the global logo black market is growing. Online dealers are cropping up, repurposing logos, and selling bootleg versions to cash-strapped start-ups at a fraction of even freelance prices.

No matter where a logo design is sold, it runs the chance of sharing traits with other designs. This doesn't necessarily require a global comprehensive search, but it does require at least some foresight from the designer. Because if you don't know whether your logo is infringing on another's design, you'll find out when you get a fancy invitation to "immediately cease and desist."

*Fly-fishing, anyone? The Fly Fishing logo design is deceptively suggestive. It offers a great example of a unique shape and form that might be descriptive, but also borders on suggestive.* PENTAGRAM

**zango**

*On the Internet, a logo design can be copied in the blink of a mouse. The Zango logo design adds protection to an already protectable name, building a large brick wall around its intellectual property.*

HORNALL ANDERSON DESIGN WORKS

**Ɗ**

**DE BEERS**

*De Beers is already facing product copycats that manufacture diamonds. Therefore, its logo design needs to be protected from knockoff brands.* THE PARTNERS

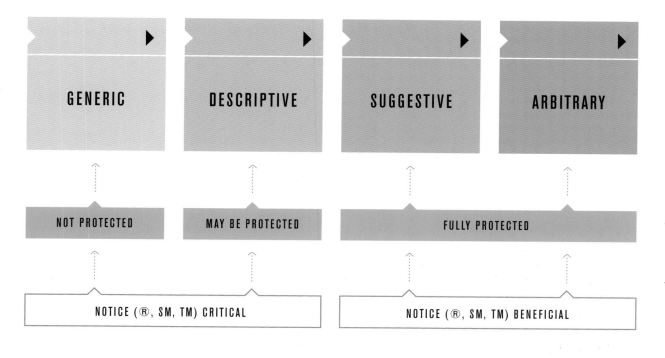

*The more generic the image, the more necessary it is to protect it legally. The descriptive side of the chart requires some form of ™ or ® to identify logo ownership. The suggestive and arbitrary sides require less protection, because the logos are distinct.*

# Technical Considerations

## JUST PUT YOUR ZIPS TOGETHER AND BLOG

For some, technology is a treat. New software launches are hailed as "events" worthy of the kind of anticipation and excitement others reserve for bat mitzvahs and rodeos. Not everyone feels this way, however. Every day, thousands of poor souls are brought to their knees by nefarious fax machines and diabolical copiers. Technology and its broad band of cohorts now run the world. Follow these technical considerations to avoid making simple mistakes within complicated media.

1. Any logo worth its price should work just as well on a golf ball as it does on a billboard.

2. Avoid using gradients or complicated techniques in the logo design. They may excite clients, but such garnishments wilt quickly under the harsh light of implementation.

3. Produce alternatives for different situations or contexts—a toolkit of pieces.

4. When it comes to using clip art or a third piece of art, as Nike's pessimistic cousin would say, "Just don't do it."

5. Design the original in vector graphics to ensure scalability without distortion. Then convert the original into all other required file formats and sizes.

6. Design a logo that works first in black and white—then add color. If a logo requires four or even five colors to convey the original idea, it is not logo. It's a circus.

7. Never lock the brand's tagline to the logo design. Advertising campaigns and taglines generally change more often than logos. Keep the logo design and tagline separate to avoid unpleasant refinements when next year's advertising campaign launches.

8. The logo should retain its integrity in a variety of media. We design in a world in which logos show up on fabric, billboards, and even space shuttles.

9. Avoid using photography. A picture is worth a thousand words, but when it comes to logos, they're worthless. Photographs are very difficult to reproduce in challenging media.

10. Be careful when using culturally sensitive images, shapes, colors, or other visual language.

Technology has a lot of toes. You'll have plenty of opportunities to step on them. Just take some time to consider the implications of each step of your logo design.

Calling the media jackals may not be smart, but organizing a golf tournament just for media is brilliant spin. Former Minnesota governor Jesse Ventura needed a logo to work on golf balls, shirts, television, and the Internet. CAPSULE

Too busy bee or not too busy bee? That is the question. The Bloom logo's black and white design is decidedly simple, comprised of monochromatic lines that are easily adaptable to varied applications.

THE PARTNERS

This logo for WhiteStar Financial Services makes the grade. The gradation works in both black and white and in color.

OCTAVO DESIGN

# **experience**engineering

*The shadow of an E reflects what isn't always visible to the consumer—the brand experience. Experience Engineering is an experience-management consulting firm.*

CAPSULE

# IMPLEM

# ENTING

DON'T BE TOO TIMID AND SQUEAMISH ABOUT YOUR ACTIONS. ALL LIFE IS AN EXPERIMENT. THE MORE EXPERIMENTS YOU MAKE, THE BETTER. – RALPH WALDO EMERSON

BOTTLE ROCKETS ARE A HEADY SOURCE OF DELIGHT FOR MANY YOUNGSTERS, FOR THE SAME REASON THEY'RE THE SOURCE OF ANGST FOR MANY PARENTS—THEY'RE UNPREDICTABLE. AS A DESIGNER, THERE'S NO TELLING WHETHER YOUR LOGO LAUNCH WILL SOAR, IMPLODE, OR SIMPLY FIZZLE. SCARY, CONSIDERING THAT NOW IT'S NOT JUST YOUR FINGERS ON THE LINE.

# Logo Launch

The digits now on the line are connected to profit margins, not hands. And the person watching over your shoulder is the client, not Mom. So if something goes wrong, you will be held accountable. As with most things in life, the best way to avoid disaster is to read instructions carefully, follow them as best you can, then hope for the best. To that end, this section's intent is to serve as an instruction manual for brand launchers.

The ideas here offer a unique perspective, along with examples of logo launches, to set you on the right course. Read on to learn more about the stages of launching a logo, specifically how to properly set expectations, identify clear objectives, orchestrate everything, and then evaluate the outcomes.

Remember, launching a logo is like planning any wedding or event. Things will go wrong. Don't panic, just stay focused.

# Potentials

## THE LOGOS WHO LAUNCH

There are plenty of ways to fail at a logo launch—more than can be covered in one book. Just look over the past decade. Amusing failures run rampant. Get your chuckle, but also try to empathize with the people behind these efforts. Just imagine yourself sitting on the wrong side of the fan when the stuff hits. If only they could have seen it coming.

A successful logo launch is not that elusive. It just requires a serious effort to build appropriate expectations, identify potential outcomes, and map out a clear plan of action.

Build expectations from the inside out. Get to the most vocal and powerful individuals internally. Take some time to get them on board. If they accept the change in an early preview, there is less chance they'll undermine it afterward. Plus, these individuals can prove loyal allies if they get excited about its potential. When launching a logo, the more allies, the better.

Potential outcomes can be varied and fairly unpredictable. Find someone who has done it before. Ask that person to review your plans and give feedback on possible outcomes.

The plan of action includes a variety of contingencies. Offer a town hall forum or an online discussion room, so employees can express their concerns or feedback. Separately, offer the same idea to external audiences. If they don't need it, cancel it. Plan for success, but don't ignore the potential for failure. Potential outcomes can be varied and fairly unpredictable. Find someone who has done it before. Ask that person to review your plans and give feedback on possible outcomes.

# TEN WAYS TO CREATE A LOGO LAUNCH BOMB

··· Launch a logo design to take attention away from or hide other issues in the business.

··· Launch the logo *on* the employees instead of *with* the employees.

··· Change the organization drastically, but make only small refinements to the logo design.

··· Change the logo design drastically, but make only small refinements to the business.

··· Change the logo design drastically, but fail to communicate the reasons internally.

··· Fail to set expectations with key people and influencers in your organization.

··· Change your logo design while facing bankruptcy protection.

··· Fail to give authentic or real answers for the change to employees.

··· Expect to have a logo design fix all your business problems and wait for the healing to begin.

··· Fight the change happening in your industry, and then play catch up with a logo design change and expect that to save your future.

## 3WIRE: LEVERAGING OPPORTUNITIES TO ENERGIZE

IMI Cornelius is a manufacturer of parts and equipment used in commercial kitchens. BEVCORe was a division of IMI Cornelius dedicated to beverage parts management. When BEVCORe acquired an outside food-service parts provider, Northern Parts United, the two entities were fused under the new name 3Wire.

During BEVCORe's transition, the management team went through a brand definition process to articulate the elements that made BEVCORe unique in the marketplace. It landed on one word: resourcefulness. The team then went through a naming process to identify a name for the new brand. The new name had to serve as the umbrella brand name for the original company; the first acquisition, Northern Parts; and any future acquisitions. The name 3Wire borrows a popular term used by fighter pilots to signal a perfect landing on an aircraft carrier.

The name 3Wire was absorbed into the logo design process, inspiring a logo that connected the precision metaphor back to the businesses' core focus. The 3 and W in the name alluded to 3Wire's parts capabilities. The logo also communicated a high-tech feel that is distinctive in an old industry not used to visible innovation. The 3Wire marketing team launched the new brand internally, and then externally, to customers a month later.

3Wire is an example of an umbrella brand successfully tying two current brands together efficiently. Existing brands that may have had equity in the marketplace are able to transition to meet the new brand, while room is made to welcome future acquisitions.

*That's one hot metaphor. The 3Wire logo is actually two sides of a heating element, represented by wires in 3 and W.* CAPSULE

The internal launch involved each and every employee. While everyone knew something was in the works, they were not all aware of the details, although the key individuals were made aware or were part of the original team. The launch was well received by Northern Parts employees and the core business partners. The launch party also garnered excitement and served to energize the staff and management team. Time will tell how all audiences adopt the new name and logo design, but early indications insinuate the changes will be leveraged with enthusiasm.

*Gather internal steam. The internal brand launch can be a highly valuable way to energize staff and get them informed and excited about the logo and its connection to them.*

# Goals and Objectives

SING IT AGAIN, PLAN

Your action plan is like a steering wheel, directing you where you need to go. Measurable goals and objectives are your mirrors. Use them periodically to check where you are. Write your goals and objectives clearly and gain agreement among the important invested parties. If you do a careful job, your client's logo will benefit later.

Typical goals and objectives include signaling a change (internally, externally, or both); communicating a list of key messages; and making messages stick with intended audiences. An important part of establishing goals is also establishing specific successes. You'll need these analytics when a client wants to know what your logo did for his or her bottom line. Don't stutter or sweat. Just reach for your analytics binder and ask if they would like to talk about it in a nearby conference room. Analytics save the day again!

Don't lose sight of the long-term results or the immeasurable affects of this change. They may seem small now, but over time they build upon themselves. For example, say you change a logo's readability, and it now translates across media more consistently. Part of the immeasurable impact here is what consistency means to your client's brand over the next 25 years. What does it say about the trust people put in your client's brand if you can consistently communicate a clear message with a new logo design? A dollar amount could be attached, but the analytics are likely too hazy for today's knowledge base.

# SAMPLE GOALS AND OBJECTIVES

··· Signal the change the brand is taking by having more than 95 percent of all internal audiences understand the change of direction.

··· Communicate the brand strategy to an energized staff and have them tell at least ten other people, internal or external.

··· Build brand equity by making sure everyone internal knows the brand promise, attributes, and personality, so they can represent the brand in our marketplace.

··· Build brand equity by ensuring that more than 60 percent of external audiences remembers the brand and associates it with the five key attributes.

··· Build brand loyalty by engaging external audiences with a new campaign started with the new logo design and communicated through an integrated campaign.

PLANNING | CREATING | **IMPLEMENTING**

DESIGN MATTERS // LOGOS 01

## THIRST: A TASTE OF IMPLEMENTATION

What sounds are capable of grooving a global village? There's no definite answer. But it never hurts to be unique. Eclectic, diverse sounds are popular staples of youth culture around the world. DJs, MCs, and producers from Los Angeles to Istanbul all have the same goal: to fill clubs. The artistry comes in the pursuit. The Heineken music contest, Thirst, was created to uncover and reward a diverse trove of hidden talents in various cities around the world, from spacey techno mix-masters to funky retro popsters.

Music and beer pair together naturally. The promotion of one often leads to more consumption of the other. The Thirst contest flew from country to country—Denmark to Croatia to Indonesia—each stop a chance to showcase that city's unique talents.

The incentive for the talent was exposure to large audiences. Audiences, in turn, got to hear fresh sounds. Heineken, a popular brand of brewed hops, got the benefit of global exposure as well as the good will of consumers and artists enjoying themselves on its tab.

The Thirst logo is a modern, bold design, consisting of the word with a directional arrow. It flexes to meet cultural circumstances, but the type and color remain consistent. The surrounding layout is organic and fresh, exemplifying the brand coming to life.

Posters, passes, coasters, fans, and whistles were just a few implementation pieces that came to live together in a visual landscape of illustrations, photographs, and type. The result is an electric, vivid brand that works across many cultures.

*The logo builds on the classic Heineken color palette, while creating a more contemporary language through the typeface and supporting hierarchy.* CRUSH

*A sexy, musical, illustrative style sets the tone of diverse surrounding materials and communications. The consistency and diversity in style is executed globally.*

The brand lives in a variety of countries. The logo therefore represents more than what the word "thirst" means in English. The logo and name adopt other anticipated and unanticipated connotations as they travel around the world.

MOST CUSTOMERS HAVE TROUBLE COMMITTING. THEY'LL TAKE HOME A JAR OF PEANUT BUTTER ONE WEEK, THEN DITCH IT FOR A CHEAPER BRAND THE NEXT. STEADY CUSTOMER LOYALTY TAKES WORK. CUSTOMERS DON'T RESPOND TO A FLOWERS-AND-CANDY SPIEL—THEY RESPOND TO BRAND CONSISTENCY.

# Consistent Flexibility

Logos are an essential part of this effort because they are part of virtually every interaction between the customer and the brand. And remember, a single message communicated seven times is always more memorable than seven messages communicated once. Beyond aesthetic and creative components, the bottom line is that logo consistency is critical.

If the devil lives in the details, then he parties in consistency. The more you explore what constitutes "consistency," the more daunting "consistent" becomes. The 3M logo is one example of consistency through color and placement. It's always a red 3M placed in a specified area of the package. Nickelodeon's logo color remains consistent, but the shape varies. Pottery Barn Kids switches out the logo shape within an icon system, but the colors (blue and gray) are always consistent. None of these is wrong. None is right. They are variations of consistency. Sounds funny, no? Nonetheless, it's an important concept to understand and consider throughout the logo design process.

If consistency equals details, flexibility equals the big picture. The amount of flexibility that lives alongside consistency is determined by the company culture. 3M's buttoned-up culture dictates that the logo has little flexibility, yet Nickelodeon's whimsical nature is reflected in a highly flexible logo design.

# Flexibility

## RUBBER DOESN'T WRINKLE

Remember Mosaic? During the Internet's spring tide from 1993 to 1996, young surfers got their feet wet with Mosaic, the first graphic Web browser. But, like the joystick and Pong, Mosaic sunk with little pomp, engulfed by the unremitting turbines of technological innovation. Few took it to heart when Mosaic folded in 1997, just five years after conception.

The moral of Mosaic is to heed change. As any surfer knows, you must adapt to the wave. Take control by giving a little of it up. Designing a logo is similar to surfing. Had Mosaic evolved as fast as the industry around it, perhaps it would still be riding high. Logos often struggle to keep pace with modern industries, especially the breakneck technology category. Prepackage flexibility into a logo design and, at the very least, it will enjoy as much longevity as possible.

A logo toolkit is a fine complement to any new logo. It's a family of options containing several logo versions that can be dropped into a variety of situations. So twenty years from now, designer John Doe Jr. will know exactly how the logo must adapt to swell onto a billboard, encircle a coffee mug, or shrink onto a pen cap.

No matter what you do, odd permutations occur and variations pop up, and there is nothing a client or design can do to prevent it completely. The toolkit is meant to provide options so this behavior is managed to a reasonable minimum. The options can cover most scenarios and then offer other options for the unknown, in the hope of covering all foreseeable situations. The key is composing a toolkit that is direct, available, and user-friendly, so designers will be more apt to use it than to gallivant off on their own short-sighted paths.

*The logo for The Society of American Fight Directors has to represent several categories. The logo flexes for specific sectors of fighting.*
CAPSULE

LUCINA winter

LUCINA spring

LUCINA summer

LUCINA fall

*Balance color and shape. The use of color as a flexible variable is common and effective for both retail brands and others needing to evoke pre-planned changes. Lucina uses color to identify seasonal updates.*

MORROW MCKENZIE

BRIGITE

BRIGITE

BRIGITE

BRIGITE

*Use shape to communicate flexibility. This opens up plenty of creative opportunities in which the logo design can tailor the brand's tone to fit certain contexts.* HARDY DESIGN

## SEED: SPREADING FLEXIBILITY AND CONSISTENCY

Communication, like science, is the process of organizing organic elements. Seed Media Group, a publisher of scientific magazines, books, and films, sought an identity that would be conceptually deep and functionally flexible. Conceptually, Sagmeister Inc. needed to make sure Seed's new logo alluded to science and media, while, functionally, it had to adapt easily to new meanings and various media.

Phyllotaxis is used in botany to describe the arrangement of leaves on stems. The form is also found in seashells, Greek architecture, highway systems, and now, Seed Media Group's logo. It's a fitting metaphor for what Seed Media Group ultimately does: organize organic elements and information. It's also a symbol of the communication process as a whole: disparate components developing out of a central axis. The result is a logo that flexes dynamically while remaining identifiably consistent.

The Seed Media Group's logo exemplifies a thoughtful approach to consistency in tone and style without a strict structure of specific logo uses. The logo exemplifies Seed Media Group's philosophy, "Science is Culture," in a way that is beautiful to any observant eye.

*Flexing the relationship between the seed icon and the logotype creates a visually stunning entrance.*

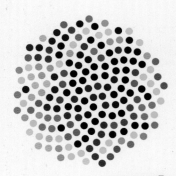

# seed media group.

*Seed Media Group's logo is simple yet has an immense depth, beauty, and flexibility.*
SAGMEISTER INC.

Don Hoyt Gorman
SENIOR EDITOR, EUROPE

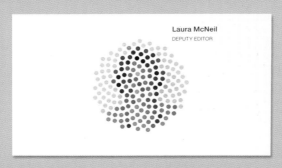

Laura McNeil
DEPUTY EDITOR

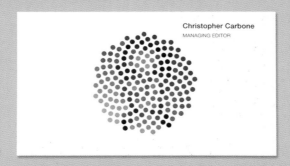

Jennifer DiBlasi
ADVERTISING/PROJECT MANAGER

Christopher Carbone
MANAGING EDITOR

*Headshots of Seed Media's staff create an intriguing mosaic on their business card and provide another interpretation of the Seed Media Group logo.*

# Style Guide

## DO THESE MAKE MY LOGO LOOK BIG?

There comes a time in every person's life when it hits. For some, it comes at work. For others, at a party. You look around the room and realize you are not the style maven you'd always taken yourself to be. With the pill of a sweater and the fade of a cuff, your style has taken a turn for the worse. Who do you turn to? If your style is dire but your pocketbook is not, you hire a professional, a stylist who knows the secrets of the cut, the potential of the hem, and the importance of the color.

As a designer, you are essentially a logo stylist. You provide suggestions that guide the client toward better logo style. However, you won't always be there. That's when your client's logo may go through some awkward phases. Understand who will be implementing your client's logo in the future and create your style guide to work for that person or team. Use the style guide to ensure your client's logo is always stylishly implemented. That's the goal.

Your style guide can use the carrot method or the stick method. The carrot rewards: "Do this right, and you are helping us build strong brand." The stick threatens: "Do this wrong, and we may have to redo your work and show you how to do it right—that won't be fun." The best style guides assume everyone wants to do right but plans for those who like to get around the rules. Make it usable and quick to read, and the majority will comply. Make it hard to understand, unnecessarily long, and hard to navigate, and you'll hear plenty of excuses.

The example subject areas are by no means exhaustive. They offer a place to start.

### BASIC SUBJECT AREAS

- ▶ Building our brand
- ▶ Product logo & versions
- ▶ Clear space & minimum size
- ▶ Colors & description of color usage
- ▶ Logo integrity & incorrect usage
- ▶ Complementary typefaces
- ▶ File name structure & color modes
- ▶ Descriptions & file formats

### ADDITIONAL SUBJECT AREAS

- ▶ Signature
- ▶ Name usage
- ▶ Tagline & symbol usage
- ▶ Secondary logo signatures
- ▶ Glossary
- ▶ Production materials
- ▶ Stationery & forms
- ▶ Communication systems & brochures

*Some brands are not producing printed guidelines anymore because the Internet is so easy to update. But, printed match color chips and printed devices such as these are also accessible to anyone, anywhere.*

CAPSULE

DESIGN MATTERS // LOGOS 01

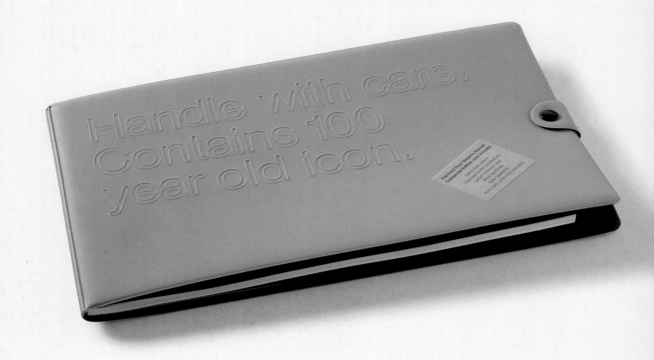

*The opening line sets the tone for the Ford logo design manual. The manual uses the automobile manual as a metaphor for taking care of an important asset. The result is engaging and thoughtful.* THE PARTNERS

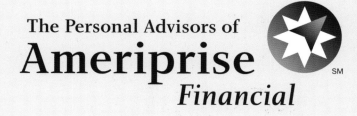

The Personal Advisors of
**Ameriprise** *Financial* SM

The Ameriprise Financial guidelines use a unique binding structure. It offers a simple, fast way to access the boundaries set up for the use of this new logo design. Designers enjoy using it, and others may find it interesting to browse through. LIPPINCOTT MERCER

# Managing Assets

## COVERING ASSETS IN A DIGITAL WORLD

You've spent months producing a highly memorable logo design. Now you need to let it go. Push it gently out of the design studio and into the big, scary world. It's an intimidating time. All your work and attention can be destroyed with a simple keystroke. Someone with a simple software package and good intentions can take your logo design and stretch it across the opening page of a presentation. Or add a drop shadow. The very tools that were necessary to create your beautiful design are the same tools that can bring it down.

The logo design's digital assets can be delivered in a variety of formats to meet specific scenarios. The key is building a structure that works for the novice user. Say a client just started to use Microsoft Word or PowerPoint and now wants to drop your new logo design into a presentation. What format does the client use? How easy is it to find that format? What size should it be? How does the client know the color will be right? Solve this confusion by considering all necessary formats available beforehand. There are formats that don't scale like .tif or .jpg, for example. Offer three size options for each.

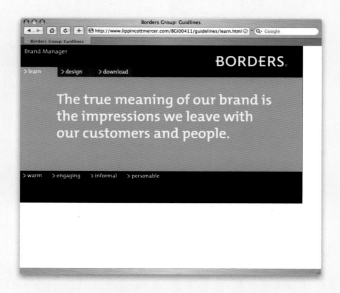

*Borders' online guide offers simple and intuitive navigation with three main sections: learn, design, and download. This format avoids overwhelming the user by condensing information.* LIPPINCOTT MERCER

Also consider the ramifications when a professional printer or other technologically savvy user needs to get something fast—they have the ability to recreate the logo if they can't find what they need, making them more dangerous than a novice. The potential exists for these users to create a new logo design that is not authentic or authorized but becomes used in more contexts.

Have the logo design available when that happens. Most people will do the right thing when they see the path in front of them. It should eliminate most future variations. If it doesn't, hire a logo cop. Logo cops don't come with a badge. They do offer a stern look and the ability to intimidate the most stalwart CEO when the time is right. Give them the authority to enforce the rules.

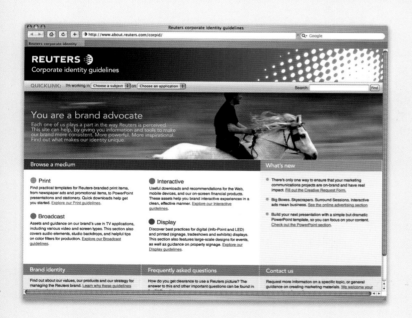

*Users can browse the Reuters site by medium: print, interactive broadcast, or display. Every time a user logs on, a brand-related message is displayed.* REUTERS

WHAT'S THE WILDEST THING YOU'VE EVER DONE? WRESTLED ALLIGATORS? LIED TO THE NURSE ABOUT YOUR WEIGHT? FOR THE SAKE OF YOUR LIMBS AND YOUR SOCIAL LIFE, LET'S HOPE IT'S IN THE MIDDLE. WHEN CREATING A LOGO, OR ANYTHING FOR THAT MATTER, A SYSTEM OF CHECKS SHOULD BALANCE CREATIVITY'S WILD EBB AND FLOW.

# Practical Considerations

For instance, be practical about the budget and timeline. Don't let things drag on, but also don't push yourself too hard. Set reasonable expectations. Designers often overextend themselves in their efforts to impress a new client. This often has the opposite effect, in the end.

It's also important for the designer to be practical, because often the client is not. Many clients have never seen the brand go through either a revolutionary or evolutionary change. You must steward clients though the design process by letting them know what is reasonable to expect. Remember, clients will judge the job you do by the expectations set forth at the beginning.

Overall, the most important function of practicality is maintaining balance between structure and creativity in the logo design. Successful logos mix beauty and information; they are artistic products that serve a practical commercial function. Make sure this is a theme of all your work.

# Budget and Timeline

## DESIGN ON THE MONEY

Managing your budget and managing your timeline are one and the same. The more time you have to work on something, the harder it is to stay on budget. The less time you have, the less budget you use. Ironically, when the budget is smaller, clients often offer you more time. The rationale is that time can make up for a deficient budget and vice versa. In fact, more time tends to strain budgets.

That said, try to get as much time as you feel you need. If you're not sure exactly how much, ask for a little extra up front. The logo shouldn't be something you rush to create. The typical timeframe for a full logo design ranges from two to eighteen months. If it takes less than two, you've likely skipped a few essential steps. If it takes more than eighteen, the world around you may have changed enough to warrant a complete restart. The time allotted for each of the steps between start and finish depends on the process you planned for your client and how the company makes design decisions. If you are working with a more democratic organization, you'll find a longer timeline is necessary to get decisions made. In the end match the process to the client culture and create a timeline that works with the process you've outlined.

The timeline is tied closely to the budget, so figure that out at the same time. Budgets can vary wildly and depend on the depth of the process: the number of people working on the design; the weeks allowed at each stage; and the number of hours in a day. A logo redesign budget can range from one or two million dollars down to ten or twenty thousand. Figure out what you need—and want. Once set, you can track results as you go. Remember, clients want to spend as little as possible. The best way to get them to spend a little more is to inform them about what they get for the money.

Now, here's the rub. Things change, as they always do. Imagine if you will: Your client finds the first round of concepts less than exciting—so you need to keep designing. How does this affect your process, timeline, and budget? Who should adjust expectations and dollar signs? You?

Your client? This depends on the process used up front and whether or not things changed on your client's side or on your side. Determine this with the client, and move forward with adjustments. Remember, the client is always right. Unless, of course, they're wrong. But if they don't admit it, you'll be left holding the bag. Getting someone to admit they're wrong is hard to do without admitting your own faults first. Open the gates of constructive communication by partly sharing responsibility for any problem. It may be hard on the ego, but it will be much softer on the process.

At the end of the entire process, it is important to go back and look at all the stages. Determine what sent the process down an alternative path. Your greatest learning will come from those challenging clients and situations that took rocky paths. Projects that go as planned are nice but are not always as satisfying, in the end. The steeper the mountain, the stronger the legs, and the better chance you'll be able to avoid the same trouble with a future client.

**PREPARATION**

## Proposal

▸ Determine budget
▸ Create project brief outlining goal
▸ Interview design firm candidates
▸ Request proposals
▸ Review and approve proposal
▸ Select internal team

**Client:** Getting a low price is not as valuable as finding a creative firm with a culture, process, talent, and experience level suited to your firm and objectives.

**Designer:** Demonstrating process and experience will get you to the table. Demonstrating passion and vision for the client's brand will go a long way toward getting work.

**PHASE ONE**

## Planning

▸ Review project brief with design firm
▸ Gather current identity materials
▸ Confirm project components and deliverables
▸ Create project schedule
▸ Conduct research
▸ Define any missing brand attributes

**Client:** Include the design team in the planning effort, involving all individuals whom you believe will impact the final results.

**Designer:** When clients don't have design experience, you can help set direction by outlining the design stages and estimating time frames for each stage.

**PHASE TWO**

## Creating

▸ Conduct logo design exploration
▸ Study applications
▸ Present logo
▸ Refine selected logo

**Client:** A constructive relationship is key to creative success. If you allow the firm creative freedom and demonstrate trust in what it will deliver, the relationship, process, and final product can only benefit.

**Designer:** Present the client with, at minimum, a couple of design options that you would be proud to implement. Once a design is chosen, refine thoughtfully, sparingly, and only when necessary.

**PHASE THREE**

## Implementing

▸ Approve layouts for implementation items
▸ Approve printing and manufacturing costs
▸ Manage production schedules
▸ Oversee printing and manufacturing
▸ Create identity standards
▸ Prepare for launch
▸ Manage and assess identity (ongoing)

**Client:** Details are small but critical. During implementation, your ability to manage details will ultimately determine whether your project stays on schedule, within budget, and faithful to the plan's original vision and objectives.

**Designer:** If you don't have experience in this area, winging it won't do. Get advice from expert vendors, mentors, peers, and partners. Because though the details you know will keep you up at night, the details you don't know will haunt you after you're done.

*Simple is the goal. The extreme complexities of a logo design process can always be simplified. Seeing the big picture is easier when you can simply see the plan, directly and forthrightly.*

# Logo Evolution
## FROM MONKEYS TO LOGO SAPIENS

Evolution and revolution. Two terms for change. Evolution is a sedate form of change. Like sap, it seeps along in thick, lazy stammers. Revolution bursts. It whips down and detonates like a twister, tossing tradition, cows, and silos high up into the storm clouds.

Revolutionary logos are effective at hailing mergers or marking the complete renovation of a damaged brand. If a company experiences major change, it makes sense that the brand and logo follow suit. A revolutionary logo is capable of altering the audience's perception of the entire brand. It should grab attention and make a definite statement about the brand's future direction.

Sometimes, however, it is better to evolve. Evolve a logo if the brand is evolving. Pretty easy to remember, but it's a bit tricky to actually pull off. Evolutionary change is subtle, but if it is so minor that it goes unnoticed, it misses the point.

Logo change is a great opportunity to gain attention and renew enthusiasm about the brand. It can signal a bright future and reflect on where the organization is going, while respecting the brand's past. It can be used to energize the client's employees, from sales staff to management to truck drivers, if employees see results at the daily level. Change can be as simple as improving morale by refreshing the corporate fleet vehicles. Give the client's sales staff a reason to reintroduce themselves to past prospects and clients by signaling organizational change; they'll likely turn it into fiscal results for themselves and the organization. Change, if managed to your client's advantage, can energize and stimulate profit.

*Evolutionary change can border on revolutionary. The change to the Wedgwood logo is significant from most perspectives. The connection between the old and new type is minimal, but the icon change is a major leap forward.* THE PARTNERS

*There are smart logos, and there are street-smart logos. The true test of any refinement is when the package joins the real world. The Wedgwood logo design hits High Street with modern appeal.* THE PARTNERS

## NURTURING GREATNESS: A ROLLING LOGO GATHERS NO MOSS

Every generation has its collection of bright starlets. Out of those, a handful of true legends emerge. They separate from the pack, meeting changing times with a fresh look while staying true to their essential beings. Is your logo a great one? Does it adapt with the times? As time passes, it's inevitable that associations get pegged onto your logo, for better or worse. And, as new mediums manifest, your logo design must not only deal with them but also must adjust to take full advantage of ever-changing surroundings.

Context changes for many reasons and can dramatically alter the logo's meaning. When the Nazis rose to power, the swastika, which had been a positive symbol in Asian, Native American, and Norse cultures for thousands of years, took on political connotations virtually overnight. The swastika is forever disfigured because the context surrounding it is as well.

Imagine if you were charged with evolving a symbol that was highly charged with negative connotations. How would you evolve the logo of a sullied company like a WorldCom or Enron to grow beyond public scandal? First, it's important to consider what is worth keeping and what should be thrown out. Approach the editing process by asking how people relate to certain components such as color, shape, and type treatment.

Then consider where the meaning manifests itself. Also, consider that changing strongly held meaning is expensive and takes time. Adopting a completely new look can be much less expensive and time-consuming for you and the client.

With any logo change, it's important to respect the equities that exist within the design. Start by understanding why the designer created it in the way he or she did. Changes to powerful equities can affect the core business if important audiences no longer identify with the brand as they did before the change.

Be sure you understand the equities that already exist in color, shape, and type or relationships between these three. Try to understand the components that are most identified by audiences and what makes the logo memorable. When refining a logo, tread carefully around equities and test results if the changes are significant enough. Although it may seem like a good idea to simplify a logo design or change it to convey a stronger metaphor, these changes may be overshadowed by what they do to existing equities. The best way to proceed is to continually look back at what was, to see how far you've come. When the distance is too far, step back. If you're not sure, test it with audiences who can understand the need for change and respect the nuances of the change.

*Byerly's gourmet grocery chain in Minnesota, USA, enjoys a long history of devoted followers who like the brand just the way it's always been. But things change. The new logo retains loyal customers and attracts new ones.* CAPSULE

*The new logo now set in context makes a contribution to the communication device. However, most consumers never consciously notice evolutionary change. That is often the idea.*

## REFINEMENTS: SACRIFICE YOUR EGO AT THE ALTER

Refinements are not just a part of the business. They are what the business is all about. You are helping the client change his or her business, by either defining or redefining the brand. When clients want refinements—oh, and they will—don't take it personally. Instead, see where the client is coming from and understand how the brand is changing.

There are five principal reasons for a brand change. They include merger and acquisition, name change, revitalization, organizational change, and functional malfunction. Often, a brand goes through several or all of these stages simultaneously. It is good to differentiate between them, because doing so will give you an idea as to what truly is the client's overall objective.

During a brand merger, two brands fuse to create a larger, third brand. The design is thus a graphic integration of the two former logos or the design of a completely new logo to embody the newly created entity. The logo design takes center stage. It's the symbol for the uniting brands.

Name change occurs for several reasons. Sometimes a perfectly nice word in one language is a very bad word in another. A new name also might be due to changing contexts that alter the meaning of the name. Or the change may be due to an internal company change. Whatever the reason, the logo design is the visual translation of the name and should help connect the new name to the brand.

Brand revitalization is usually driven by changes in the surrounding industry or cultures. Industries can change quickly and can make a mature logo appear tired. Revitalization can breathe new life into the brand and signal fresh energy to important audiences, both internal and external.

Organizational change is a new brand direction. It is a core change that often takes place when the brand is entering a new global or domestic market. This kind of change requires significant resources and entails significant risk. It also requires a signal to the internal and external community that change is flowing outward from within the organization. A logo refinement signals this new direction. It is a rally point for internal audiences to begin the effort to set a new course.

In some cases, logos change not because the organization changed but because the logo just never really worked well in the first place. There is no special term for that. It's a common problem, especially among small-business clients. Startups with small budgets often initially invest little in the logo. As the business grows and becomes more sophisticated, a new logo suits the business better.

# JOHN DEERE

1876

1912

1936

1937

1950

1956

1968

*The evolution of the John Deere logo exemplifies change on a number of levels. Most notably, the logo is tailored to fit international audiences and is stylistically simplified.* DEERE & COMPANY

# Steward the Design Process

ONE PART MAGIC, ONE PART SAUSAGE

A lot of odd metaphors describe the inside of the creative process. Some people compare the creative process to the inside of a sausage factory. Others compare it to magic. Sausages are a bit too processed, magic is a bit too undisciplined. Neither represents exactly what the creative process is all about.

The challenge of any creative process lies in not getting discouraged or settling when ideas aren't flowing quickly. Sometimes it happens right away. Other times it seems to take an eternity. Often the problem is lack of inspiration. For instance, coming up with a memorable logo design for a name that is boring, descriptive, and five words long can be endlessly challenging. Coming up with a design for a product with a name like YANK can be less challenging, because the name is energetic, vivid, and unique. The better the inputs, the less time the creative process should take, and the better the output on the other side.

Managing a process with so many variables sounds about as easy as trapping excited worms in a can. It's definitely not for the faint of heart. It helps to find an approach that suits you. Some state the problem and ask for solutions. Others give creatives the facts and see what happens. However you approach it, keep your team inspired. Most problems have obvious solutions; eliminate those in advance. This sometimes creates constraints, which is good. Time, budget, and other parameters can also add constraints and can serve as tremendous motivation to achieving creative output.

*These are some real, well-meaning quotes from clients who were attempting to keep the design process on track.*

"Are you sure we couldn't use something that looks kind of like Disney's logo?"

Can you add a drop shadow or a cool bevel to the logo?"

"I like this logo, but let me take it home and show my wife. She's the artist in the family."

"We'd like to run a contest where our employees come up with the design for our logo."

"I'd like to be able to see my logo from an airplane."

"Could you match the logo color to my bedroom walls?"

"I love them all…can you combine concept one and two with the type of concept three?"

"Can we put these logo designs in the Student Union for everyone to vote?"

# CASE S

# TUDIES

THE MANNER OF AN ARTIST IS ESSENTIALLY
INDIVIDUAL; THE METHOD OF AN ARTIST
IS ABSOLUTELY UNIVERSAL. THE FIRST IS
PERSONALITY, WHICH NO ONE SHOULD
COPY; THE SECOND IS PERFECTION, WHICH
ALL SHOULD AIM AT.  – OSCAR WILDE

| THE CLIENT: | RED WING SHOES |
| TIME FRAME: | SIX MONTHS |
| DESIGN FIRM: | CAPSULE (USA) |

# Red Wing Shoes

## THE MOST AMAZING THING YOU'VE NEVER SEEN

### INTRODUCTION

Red Wing Shoes' identity is a logo heard around the world. What is now Red Wing Shoe Company, Inc., began with modest means and grew to become an international brand of handmade work boots and fashionable footwear. The classic work boots brand has widely become a fashion boot as well.

Capsule, a brand development and design firm based in Minneapolis, USA, redesigned the brand's logo. The effort had to tie into a larger brand evolution that was taking place simultaneously. This meant the logo required extensive planning aimed at transforming the logo's functional elements and retaining its existing brand equities. Red Wing Shoes' authentic American style is based on its decades of heritage—Norman Rockwell immortalized the brand in a series of drawings from 1960 to1969—and its role as a figurehead of old-fashioned quality.

### PLANNING

Planning included the exhaustive research and study of similar changes implemented by brands such as Shell, Harley-Davidson, John Deere, and many others. At this stage, research suggested much of the logo's equity resided in the black type over the red wing. Moderate variations lost the authentic American feel that attracted consumers in Canada, Mexico, Europe, and Asia. This planning process set the foundation for the design's direction and exploration.

EST. 1905

# RED WING SHOES

®

*The Red Wing Shoes wing logo, with an overlay of the Red Wing Shoes name, was originally designed in 1904.*

*Remove the type from the wing, and it morphs into a "box of pork chops" that doesn't offer an ideal solution.*

*The revised Red Wing Shoes logo varies from the original, but the untrained eye is challenged to see the difference.*

## CREATING

The process of visualizing and creating change was driven by both client and design teams with an ability to flex the design process. It began with an exhaustive exploration of possibilities that helped the group visualize change. Studies were conducted to observe the shapes of various wings. The original swan wing was the model. Type studies were also conducted to ensure that the style remained similar enough to the original. The new design improved readability and other details, such as consistent thick and thins. A toolkit was also designed to provide a variety of options for use in specific contexts. The design was refined, and the wing was hand-drawn more than ten times throughout the process.

© 2007 Red Wing Shoe Company

## IMPLEMENTING

An exhaustive online site was created for vendors to source the redesigned Red Wing Shoes logo and toolkit. The new logo was implemented on everything from signage and advertising to shoes and other clothing accessories. The result was a logo design that offers a multitude of options with a logo toolkit and design that retain original brand equity.

*A redrawn wing spurred the creation of a toolkit of Red Wing Shoes logo designs. Each solution makes a connection back to the original but offers flexibility for specific media.*

# Royal Tropical Institute

BRANCHING OUT

## INTRODUCTION

The Royal Tropical Institute (KIT) is an international center of knowledge and expertise focusing on international and intercultural cooperation. The organization contributes its energy to building sustainable development, alleviating poverty, and preserving and promoting diverse cultures. Though KIT has roots in the Netherlands, its reach is global.

## PLANNING

Eden Design & Communication used nature as inspiration when designing the Royal Tropical Institute's new logo. The result is a visual expression of KIT's mission and core values conveyed in a bright, organic form. At the heart of the design process was KIT's brand promise: knowledge, choices, and opportunities.

KIT needed a logo that would inspire others to provide their support. To do this, the logo needed to express KIT's mission—assisting people in developing countries—while also conveying its most essential values of equivalence, diversity, sustainable development, and good government. The goal was to strike a non-Western, worldly, dignified, cooperative, sharing, and respectful design tone, one of an ambassador with the welcoming cadence of a friendly, trusted acquaintance. The logo also had to engage others on a fundamental level so the audience would become curious and motivated to learn more.

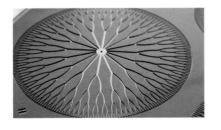

*The designer gathered tree images from all over the world with the goal of creating a universally recognizable, relevant, and organic image. The influence of these initial tree images can be seen in the final logo.*

*The Royal Tropical Institute's logo organically blends people and trees into a unique, simple, and memorable design.*

## CREATING

Eden Design went through a thorough planning process to build a strong and clear foundation; it then used this foundation to leap into the organic creative process, which followed many paths. By conducting an exhaustive visual image study, the designers found the right metaphors to convey this complex and sensitive message.

Because the Institute increases choices and spreads a broader worldview, contributing to the odds of a better life, one design inspiration was the tree of life, an ancient symbol with many iterations and interpretations. In the search for the correct tree form, the design team explored many variations. In the end, however, Eden's innovative and visually compelling design integrated human forms, which reflect the organization's worldly focus. For color, Eden chose a non-Western, worldly, and respectful color palette.

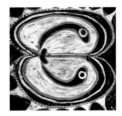

*To develop the identity's color palette, the design team collected art and imagery from specific world regions as inspiration.*

*Refinements to the logo illustrate how the two elements gracefully come together.*

## IMPLEMENTING

The Royal Tropical Institute's goal was to generate and disseminate specialized knowledge in the areas of sustainable economic development, education, healthcare, and culture. This information would be distributed through a variety of channels, meaning the company needed tailored logo variations for different groups and initiatives. The new logo also needed to reflect the organization's values by creating a flexible, structured hierarchy. There were many challenges in this project, but careful research and attention to every element, as well as understanding how the overall program held together, paid off.

Eden Design's implementation of the larger visual language was impeccably detailed, and the logo beautifully reflects the organization's mission, personality, and brand promise. The resulting logo design is aligned accurately with the organization's vision and executed with flawless detail.

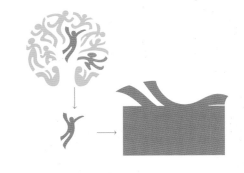

*The logo design is the center of an elegant, efficient, and global design system.*

THE CLIENT: LONDON SYMPHONY ORCHESTRA

TIME FRAME: FOUR MONTHS

DESIGN FIRM: THE PARTNERS (UNITED KINGDOM)

# London Symphony Orchestra

AN INSTITUTION CHANGES ITS TUNE

## INTRODUCTION

The London Symphony Orchestra logo was redesigned to reflect recent organizational changes. The redesign represents the elegant and delicate balance between the orchestra and the conductor. It's a visual depiction of the two parties working in concert to create a memorable musical experience.

The Partners, a design consultancy based in the United Kingdom, designed the new logo for the world-renowned institution. The firm's process included three distinct stages that eventually brought vibrant life to the combined vision of the organization and the design team.

## PLANNING

The addition of a new performance venue, LSO St. Luke's, was the most notable of several new changes that impacted the London Symphony Orchestra, its employees, and its patrons. It therefore seemed like the appropriate time to signal the changes in a substantial way. When The Partners took on the project, they began by gathering research and inspiration about where the organization was heading. The team delved deeply into the world of classical music, gathering firsthand research from behind the curtain. This work informed the creative brief for the new visual identity.

*The establishment of a new performance venue, LSO St. Luke's, London, is a significant change that propels the logo redesign.*

The line between letters and image blur together in a new logo. The illustration of a conductor is also a monogram, lending warmth and humanity to the London Symphony Orchestra.

## CREATING

The design of the LSO logo blended an elegant, casually handwritten version of the organization's acronym with a subtle reference to the conductor. This final identity was the product of an exploratory design process that led designers down a number of paths pointing to the past, present, and future history of the organization.

The new logo signaled changes, including the addition of a new location that would be the new home of free public lunchtime concerts, new community events, and a variety of other concerts. Beyond this, the new identity set a tone for the orchestra's future. The final test was the presentation of the final logo design to the full orchestra. The musicians' collective tapping of their instruments symbolized approval and hailed the beginning of a new era.

*Orchestra players are a key audience that the design team needs to impress. The symbolic tapping of their instruments signals approval, a key element of future success.*

## IMPLEMENTING

The new visual identity was implemented on a variety of media and communication tools. It was executed on vehicle sides, on the organization's website, in campaign advertisements, on programs, on live concert CD covers, and throughout other supplemental materials. The final product heralded change while paying homage to a rich history.

*The integration of the new logo into a seasonal campaign can be a good test to see whether results show up in the fiscal column. In this case, online ticket and CD sales went up 200 percent.*

THE CLIENT: SPRINT

TIME FRAME: TWO MONTHS

DESIGN FIRM: LIPPINCOTT MERCER (USA)

# Sprint

## ELEGANTLY MERGING TWO BRANDS

### INTRODUCTION

When Sprint and Nextel planned to merge, the focus was on creating America's premier communications company. Nextel benefited from public awareness of the Sprint brand, both its history of innovation and asset value. But the new logo design also had to represent Nextel and its brand equities. Design firm Lippincott Mercer created a new logo for the new telecommunications brand.

### PLANNING

The merger of two highly recognized and respected brands required thoughtful planning and strategy. Because of the competitive nature of the visual landscape, extensive research was essential. Each existing logo's equity had to be measured carefully and then carried forward, with one name and style taking a dominant position.

Logo

Logo

Pin

Finish Line

*It's red, yellow, and abstract all over. Both brands have equity in their names, color, and visual shapes. The design team chose to leverage the yellow of Nextel and the pin drop of Sprint.*

Color

Color

# Sprint®

*Sprint's new logo flies high. It's a simple, beautiful, and memorable design, representing both the classic pin drop and a new wing in flight.*

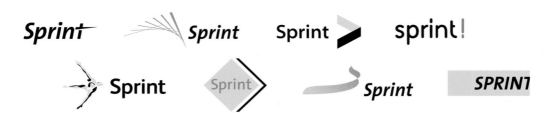

*Exploration has many faces. After the company decides to keep the Sprint name, designers look at a variety of ways to integrate the equities of both brands through shape, color, and typography.*

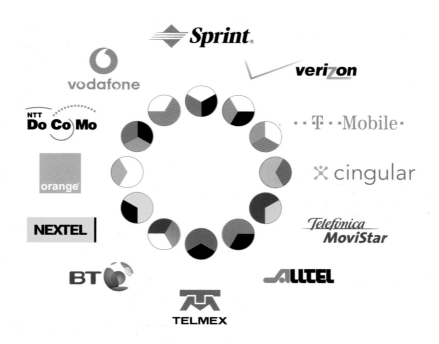

*The communications category is chock full of color. Designers conduct a thorough and simple audit to clearly identify what color palette the new Sprint logo can own in a crowded marketplace.*

## CREATING

Creativity rarely escapes a corporate board meeting without a few substantial bruises. The new logo design for Sprint defies most expectations for a large corporate logo design. It is not only an effective logo on a functional level; it is also inspired in form. The metaphor of the pin drop, a trademarked sound for Sprint, elegantly matches the shape of a wing taking flight. The logo design sets Sprint in the only open spot on a cluttered map of competitors in the telecommunications industry, which many suits said couldn't be done at this point in the history of the category. Most important, it positions Sprint in the minds of consumers in a far more effective manner than most of the competitive set.

## IMPLEMENTING

Some logo designs almost execute themselves. This often occurs when they've been designed carefully from the beginning. The new Sprint logo went through an efficient implementation in a variety of media, crossing over into signage, the Web, advertisements, and even backpacks. The new brand vision is refreshing on many levels, alluding to better customer relationships and a bright future.

*When you are Sprint, the launch of a new logo turns a few heads. Whether it's a topic of conversation, confusion, or it's an afterthought, the new Sprint logo touches millions of consumers.*

# Kinderarzt, Dr. Uhlig

MAKING KIDS SMILE

## INTRODUCTION

Dr. Uhlig's practice is concerned with healing children and helping children feel comfortable in an unfamiliar and discomforting situation, such as in a doctor's office. The logo plays an important role in this effort.

Factor Design, of Hamburg, Germany, worked with the doctor to create a logo that would convey a cheerful tone. The challenge was to make the logo welcoming for young children without going over the top in the eyes of parents or older children.

## PLANNING

Doctors can be intimidating, instruments can be intimidating, and the combination can make a standard checkup a traumatic experience for many adults, let alone children. The planning process, also called a "launch," for Dr. Uhlig's new logo design focused on comforting a very specific section of his practice: his youngest patients. Success required equal participation from the client, Dr. Uhlig, as well as the design firm. The new design needed to reflect a medical professional and also needed to engage and welcome children. The team was set to create, brief in hand.

# KINDERARZT

## Doktor Uhlig

*The logo for Dr. Uhlig's medical practice, Kinderarzt, reinvents the tone of both his brand and his stethoscope. The medical device that is traditionally used to listen to patients' heartbeats appears in this context as the personification of cheer and happiness.*

*Factor Design lets research inspire. The design team has children draw images of doctor's artifacts and the surroundings at the doctor's office. The result is a better understanding of their perspective. Copies of original art are used on a variety of communications.*

*Certain applications require a fresh outlook. Stationery is used and seen almost exclusively by parents. Therefore, it must address their needs while remaining true to the original kid-friendly concept.*

## CREATING

The design process absorbed inspiration from children's drawings, industry artifacts, and a variety of other inputs. Out of this, the design process homed in on one concept: creating a smiling face with a stethoscope. The idea garnered rave reviews from the clinic and the rest of the team. After that, colors were chosen to convey warmth while still communicating professionalism. In the end, primary colors were chosen to appeal to the young audience.

Many children's practices pepper waiting rooms with teddy bears and clowns that distract kids momentarily but don't lend warmth to the environment at a fundamental level. Other practices simply approach kids in the same way they would adults. The results can feel cold, sterile, and intimidating. The new Kinderarzt logo conveys friendliness and care in a light, unique, and clever way.

## IMPLEMENTING

The logo design inspired the rest of the project, from the kids' waiting area to a variety of other communications. Childlike energy bounced out clearly from the patterns created from original kids' drawings. The color palette was simple, playful, and never intimidating.

When kids are involved, there is extra incentive to create something inspirational. The new logo is an effort to do just that. The final logo achieves this in many ways, becoming a popular conversation piece that the audience also uses functionally and values aesthetically.

*The logo design and surrounding language have to communicate in a digital world— a place where some children may be more comfortable than their parents.*

| THE CLIENT: | (RED)™ |
| TIME FRAME: | TWO MONTHS |
| DESIGN FIRM: | WOLFF OLINS (USA) |

# (RED)™

## THE COLOR OF COMMERCE, EMERGENCY, AND SOCIAL CONSCIOUSNESS

### INTRODUCTION

Conceptualized by Bono, (RED) is an idea—an idea that connects brands with conscious commerce, by making the idea of "doing good" real and fiscally rewarding. It provides a financial impetus for prominent brands to lend their clout to bettering humanity.

### PLANNING

The design team was given the direction to create a brand that would exemplify "doing good is good business" and bring to life this idea. The design needed to entice big, powerful brands by standing apart from the myriad other organizations requesting financial support. The concept of (RED) needed to build its own equity by borrowing from the equity of iconic brands. According to (RED)'s lead strategist, Sam Wilson, "(RED) is an extraordinary union of business, people, and ideas, a twenty-first–century brand that inspires individuals, drives positive commerce, and advances the world. All profits go to the global fund to fight AIDS, tuberculosis, and malaria in Africa."

The direction and inspiration were set. The next task was to create a logo design to exemplify the idea: a design that created urgency of attention and also provided enough exposure to partner brands to interest them in joining the cause.

*Just as (RED) borrows equity from famous brands, it also borrows equity from culturally valuable words.*

# (RED)™

*(RED) is a brand created for social good. It's a brand designed for global advancement, blending commerce and charity.*

## CREATING

The challenge was how to unite two brands visually. The traditional method of bonding two brands—simply placing them side by side—didn't seem to live up to the aspirations of the brand. The brand needed to covet the generous partner brands but not lose its own individual equity. Striking a balance between the two was difficult.

The design explorations led the team to a simple, elegant idea. Two brackets surround the word red. When shown with a collaborative brand, the mark is embraced "to the power of (RED)." Minimalist in visual and conceptual form, the design is metaphorical. As you dig, it tells more of the brand's story. Further, the design is naturally unique. All three criteria are not just met but exemplified with a logo design destined to become a force of economic and social inspiration.

# (PRODUCT)RED™

# DO THE (RED) THING™

*By surrounding other logo designs, (RED)'s logo creates a visual relationship that is both comforting and clear. The result is a brand relationship that creates curiosity in both the new and existing brands.*

## IMPLEMENTING

If you have earned airline miles in the past twenty years, you've interacted with a loyalty program. Designed to buy loyalty, these programs have grown up to become ugly beasts, creating large corporate liabilities and disillusioned consumers. The implementation of (RED) marks the beginning of something new, a method of earning consumer loyalty instead of attempting to buy it—earning it by proving loyalty to customers, to the Earth, to employees, and to the global community.

By surrounding existing brands with the (RED) brand, the implementation should provide the inspiration and even provide the vehicle for leading brands to take ownership of a new philosophy around earned consumer loyalty. Implemented and accepted by the marketplace, this new brand aims to breed more conscious consumers.

*The card is designed to use everyday transactions to purchase a piece of global responsibility. The (RED) card paints a brand with the passion surrounding responsible living without the guilt.*

*This generated image sets the (RED) logo in context, showing how the brand would look dropped into global media hot spot Times Square.*

# LOGO G

# ALLERY

WHAT IS ALL WISDOM SAVE A COLLECTION
OF PLATITUDES? BUT THE MAN WHO ORDERS
HIS LIFE ACCORDING TO THEIR TEACHINGS
CANNOT GO FAR WRONG.
– NORMAN DOUGLAS

**First Citizens**

1.

2.

3.

4.

5.

6.

1. CLIENT: FIRST CITIZENS BANK FIRM: LIPPINCOTT MERCER (USA) DESIGNERS: JULIA MCGREEVY, BRENDAN MURPHY, KEVIN HAMMOND ART DIRECTOR: CONNIE BIRDSALL  2. CLIENT: TOURISTEES.COM FIRM: TIM FRAME DESIGN (USA) DESIGNER: TIM FRAME ART DIRECTOR: TIM FRAME 3. CLIENT: GOODYS PAINT COMPANY FIRM: A3 DESIGN (USA) DESIGNER: AMANDA ALTMAN ART DIRECTOR: ALAN ALTMAN  4. CLIENT: DEBRETT'S LIMITED FIRM: THE PARTNERS (UK) DESIGNER: BOB YOUNG ART DIRECTOR: NINA JENKINS  5. CLIENT: DIRECTV FIRM: INTERBRAND (USA) DESIGNER: DZUNG TRAN ART DIRECTOR: TODD TRUE  6. CLIENT: HOST MARRIOT FIRM: CHUTE GERDEMAN (USA) DESIGNER: TIM FRAME ART DIRECTOR: TIM FRAME

7.

8.

hamilton
international

9.

10.

ELYSIUM
WEDDING PRODUCTIONS

11.

12.

7. CLIENT: BRAINTREE DEVELOPMENT GROUP FIRM: SOCKEYE CREATIVE (USA) DESIGNERS: PETER METZ, KURT HOLLOMON ART DIRECTOR: PETER METZ 8. CLIENT: VAJA FIRM: RDYA DESIGN GROUP (ARGENTINA) DESIGNER: RICARDO DRAB ART DIRECTOR: RICARDO DRAB 9. CLIENT: HAMILTON INTERNATIONAL AIRPORT FIRM: CUNDARI SFP (CANADA) DESIGNER: MIKE KWAN ART DIRECTOR: MIKE KWAN 10. CLIENT: JAGUAR FIRM: THE PARTNERS (UK) DESIGNERS: STEVE OWEN, HELEN COOLEY ART DIRECTOR: GREG QUINTON 11. CLIENT: TOWER 23 HOTEL FIRM: HOLLIS BRAND COMMUNICATIONS (USA) DESIGNER: DON HOLLIS ART DIRECTOR: DON HOLLIS 12. CLIENT: ELYSIUM FIRM: MATTSON CREATIVE (USA) DESIGNER: TY MATTSON ART DIRECTOR: TY MATTSON

1.

2.

3.

4.

5.

6.

1. CLIENT: ELEPHANT PHARMACY FIRM: TACTIX CREATIVE, INC. (USA) DESIGNER: PAUL HOWALT ART DIRECTORS: PAUL HOWALT, CABELL HARRIS
2. CLIENT: GAME CRAZY FIRM: SOCKEYE CREATIVE (USA) DESIGNERS: PETER METZ, ROBERT WEES ART DIRECTOR: PETER METZ 3. CLIENT: IDEAPARK
LTD FIRM: HAHMO DESIGN LTD (FINLAND) DESIGNERS: ANTTI RAUDASKOSKI, PEKKA PIIPPO ART DIRECTOR: ANTTI RAUDASKOSKI 4. CLIENT: GUINCO
FIRM: AIJALON (USA) DESIGNER: JILL ANDREASEN ART DIRECTOR: LANCE FORD 5. CLIENT: EMAZEMENT FIRM: WOLKEN COMMUNICA (USA)
DESIGNER: RYAN BURLINSON ART DIRECTOR: KURT WOLKEN 6. CLIENT: URBAN BLUEPRINT FIRM: CAPSULE (USA) DESIGNER: DAN BAGGENSTOSS
ART DIRECTOR: BRIAN ADDUCCI

7.

8.

9.

10.

11.

12.

DESIGN MATTERS // LOGOS 01

7. CLIENT: NATWEST BANK FIRM: THE PARTNERS (UK) DESIGNERS: NINA JENKINS, KATE HUTCHISON, TRACY AVISON, NICK EAGLETON, KEVIN LAN ART DIRECTORS: GILL THOMAS, TONY DE STE CROIX  8. CLIENT: CARIHOME FIRM: MIND CORPORATION (USA) DESIGNER: ANDREW KING ART DIRECTOR: ANDREW ROBINSON  9. CLIENT: VODAFONE FIRM: ENTERPRISE IG (UK) DESIGNERS: JAN ENKELMANN, LISA CARRANA ART DIRECTOR: GIANNI TOZZI 10. CLIENT: BALL HAWG FIRM: RICKABAUGH GRAPHICS (USA) DESIGNER: DAVE CAP ART DIRECTOR: ERIC RICKABAUGH 11. CLIENT: WAGS FIRM: URBAN INFLUENCE DESIGN STUDIO (USA) DESIGNERS: MICHAEL MATES, HENRY YIU ART DIRECTOR: HENRY YIU 12. CLIENT: MENDOTA HOMES FIRM: ADSOKA (USA) DESIGNER: GRETCHEN WESTBROCK ART DIRECTOR: GRETCHEN WESTBROCK

McCLELLAND & STEWART

1.

2.

3.

4.

5.

6.

1. CLIENT: MCCLELLAND AND STEWART FIRM: CUNDARI SFP (CANADA) DESIGNER: CLEA FORKERT ART DIRECTOR: PAUL HODGSON 2. CLIENT: OASEN FIRM: TOTAL IDENTITY BV (THE NETHERLANDS) DESIGNER: LÉON STOLK ART DIRECTOR: LÉON STOLK 3. CLIENT: LEAP FROG-FLY/TEMPLIN BRINK FIRM: GLITSCHKA STUDIOS (USA) DESIGNER: VON R. GLITSCHKA ART DIRECTOR: JOEL TEMPLIN 4. CLIENT: 59 LIMOUSINE FIRM: URBAN INFLUENCE DESIGN STUDIO (USA) DESIGNERS: MICHAEL MATES, HENRY YIU ART DIRECTOR: HENRY YIU 5. CLIENT: HOPE TO GO FIRM: ROME & GOLD CREATIVE (USA) DESIGNER: LORENZO ROMERO ART DIRECTOR: ROBERT E. GOLDIE 6. CLIENT: BAGBY AND COMPANY FIRM: UNIT-Y (USA) DESIGNER: ANDREY NAGORNY ART DIRECTOR: ANDREY NAGORNY

**YELLOWPAGES.COM**™

**eden**
Natural Market

7.

8.

BOWLING GREEN
FALCONS™

*Spanish Walk*

9.

10.

allc⏻nnect

deRuiter
creating flower business

11.

12.

7. CLIENT: YELLOWPAGES.COM FIRM: INTERBRAND (USA) DESIGNER: MALCOLM STEWARD ART DIRECTOR: TODD TRUE  8. CLIENT: EDEN NATURAL MARKET FIRM: MACMILLAN LYNCH (CANADA) DESIGNER: KERRY LYNCH ART DIRECTOR: KERRY LYNCH 9. CLIENT: BOWLING GREEN FIRM: RICKABAUGH GRAPHICS (USA) DESIGNER: DAVE CAP ART DIRECTOR: ERIC RICKABAUGH 10. CLIENT: TAYLOR WOODROW HOMES FIRM: MATTSON CREATIVE (USA) DESIGNER: TY MATTSON ART DIRECTOR: TY MATTSON 11. CLIENT: ALLCONNECT FIRM: HORNALL ANDERSON DESIGN WORKS (USA) DESIGNERS: JAMES TEE, TIFFANY PLACE, YURI SHVETS, SONJA MAX, BELINDA BOWLING, STEPHANIE COOPER ART DIRECTORS: JACK ANDERSON, JAMES TEE 12. CLIENT: DE RUITER FIRM: TOTAL IDENTITY (THE NETHERLANDS) DESIGNER: ANDRÉ MOL ART DIRECTOR: ANDRÉ MOL

INTELSAT.

BURLWOOD
FINANCIAL GROUP, INC.

1.

2.

MARKS|MARKUS inc.

3.

4.

Segen

5.

6.

1. CLIENT: INTELSAT FIRM: SIEGEL & GALE (USA) DESIGNERS: JOHNNY LIM, DAVID WEISS, STEVE KIM ART DIRECTOR: JUSTIN PETERS
2. CLIENT: BURLWOOD FINANCIAL GROUP FIRM: CAPSULE (USA) DESIGNER: DAN BAGGENSTOSS ART DIRECTOR: BRIAN ADDUCCI
3. CLIENT: MARKUS INC. FIRM: SEGURA, INC. (USA) DESIGNER: RYAN HALVORSEN ART DIRECTOR: CARLOS SEGURA 4. CLIENT: MPIRE
FIRM: TURNSTYLE (USA) DESIGNER: BEN GRAHAM ART DIRECTOR: BEN GRAHAM 5. CLIENT: SEGEN FIRM: ONE BRAND GROUP (UK)
DESIGNER: MARC FRENCH ART DIRECTOR: MARC FRENCH 6. CLIENT: PROMOMEDIA GROUP FIRM: IRIDIUM + KOLEGRAM (CANADA)
DESIGNER: DAVID DAIGLE ART DIRECTOR: JEAN-LUC DENAT

7.

8.

**MasterCard**
Worldwide

9.

10.

11.

12.

7. CLIENT: CITY PACIFIC LAW FIRM FIRM: OCTAVO DESIGN PTY LTD (AUSTRALIA) DESIGNER: GARY DOMONEY ART DIRECTOR: GARY DOMONEY
8. CLIENT: OLYMPIC STATIONERY PRODUCTS FIRM: SPARK STUDIO PTY LTD (AUSTRALIA) DESIGNER: TONY ALBERS ART DIRECTOR: SEAN PETHICK
9. CLIENT: MASTERCARD WORLDWIDE FIRM: FUTUREBRAND (USA) DESIGNERS: MICHELLE MATTHEWS, CHRIS SIARKIEWICZ ART DIRECTOR: WALLACE
KRANTZ 10. CLIENT: GATORBACK FIRM: CAPSULE (USA) DESIGNER: DAN BAGGENSTOSS ART DIRECTOR: BRIAN ADDUCCI 11. CLIENT: RADARGOLF
FIRM: Y&R (USA) DESIGNER: CHRIS ROONEY ART DIRECTOR: CHRIS ROONEY 12. CLIENT: CAN FIRM: FACTOR DESIGN (GERMANY) DESIGNER: TOBIAS
HEIDMEIER ART DIRECTOR: JOHANNES ERLER

1.

2.

systemtrans®

3.

4.

5.

6.

1. CLIENT: GRAVITY FLOORING FIRM: THE PARTNERS (UK) DESIGNERS: STEVE OWEN, JAMES HARVEY, KATE SHEPHERD, LEON BAHRANI
ART DIRECTOR: NINA JENKINS 2. CLIENT: IBM POWER LOCK/FRESH ID FIRM: GLITSCHKA STUDIOS (USA) DESIGNER: VON R. GLITSCHKA
ART DIRECTOR: KRISTI SADLER 3. CLIENT: SYSTEMTRANS FIRM: 28 LIMITED BRAND (GERMANY) DESIGNER: MIRCO KURTH ART DIRECTOR: MIRCO
KURTH 4. CLIENT: OCT GROUP, CHINA FIRM: ENTERPRISE IG (CHINA) DESIGNERS: ERIC SHUM, MICHAEL CHIANG ART DIRECTOR: TK WONG
5. CLIENT: ANIMAL ADVENTURE FIRM: CAPSULE (USA) DESIGNER: DAN BAGGENSTOSS ART DIRECTOR: BRIAN ADDUCCI 6. CLIENT: POSTSPEED
ENVELOPE PAPER FIRM: SPARK STUDIO PTY LTD (AUSTRALIA) DESIGNER: ADAM PUGH ART DIRECTOR: SEAN PETHICK

7.

8.

9.

10.

11.

12.

7. CLIENT: TIAXA FIRM: SEGURA, INC. (USA) DESIGNER: CARLOS SEGURA ART DIRECTOR: CARLOS SEGURA  8. CLIENT: PALADIN FIRM: CAPSULE (USA) DESIGNER: DAN BAGGENSTOSS ART DIRECTOR: BRIAN ADDUCCI 9. CLIENT: DR. KOEPCHEN FIRM: 28 LIMITED BRAND (GERMANY) DESIGNER: MIRCO KURTH ART DIRECTOR: MIRCO KURTH 10. CLIENT: TRENDSPHERE LLC FIRM: ENVISION+ (GERMANY) DESIGNER: PROF. BRIAN SWITZER ART DIRECTOR: PROF. BRIAN SWITZER 11. CLIENT: SPRINGBOK FIRM: OXIDE DESIGN CO. (USA) DESIGNERS: DREW DAVIES, JOE SPARANO, BILL BOLLMAN ART DIRECTOR: DREW DAVIES 12. CLIENT: CREDIT SUISSE FIRM: ENTERPRISE IG (ENGLAND) DESIGNERS: GLENN TUTSSEL, JOHAN ENGELBRECHT ART DIRECTOR: GLENN TUTSSEL

1.

2.

FASHION AT WORK
CORONET

3.

4.

5.

6.

1. CLIENT: SURVEY & BALLOT SYSTEMS FIRM: CAPSULE (USA) DESIGNER: HEATHER WEISS ART DIRECTOR: BRIAN ADDUCCI 2. CLIENT: LYRIS FIRM: HARDY DESIGN LTD. (BRAZIL) DESIGNERS: BRUNO SOUZA, MARIANA HARDY ART DIRECTOR: MARIANA HARDY 3. CLIENT: CORONET FIRM: WHITERHINO (AUSTRALIA) DESIGNERS: ANDREW TIBB, JEREMY TIBB, PETER BINEK ART DIRECTOR: ANDREW TIBB 4. CLIENT: HANARO TELECOM FIRM: TOTAL IDENTITY (THE NETHERLANDS) DESIGNER: ANDRÉ MOL ART DIRECTOR: ANDRÉ MOL 5. CLIENT: AKATHERM FIRM: ONE BRAND GROUP (UK) DESIGNER: CARL SALIBA ART DIRECTOR: CARL SALIBA 6. CLIENT: MORTGAGE SELECTION SERVICES FIRM: OCTAVO DESIGN PTY LTD (AUSTRALIA) DESIGNER: GARY DOMONEY ART DIRECTOR: GARY DOMONEY

™ EMBARQ™

easywell

7.

8.

Parametric™

HANDI
MEDICAL SUPPLY

9.

10.

SwissLife

compellent

11.

12.

7. CLIENT: EMBARQ FIRM: SALT BRANDING (USA) DESIGNER: CÉSAR CHIN ART DIRECTOR: PAUL PARKIN  8. CLIENT: EASYWELL SOLUTIONS FIRM: ONE
BRAND GROUP (UK) DESIGNER: CARL SALIBA ART DIRECTOR: CARL SALIBA  9. CLIENT: PARAMETRIC FIRM: TURNSTYLE (USA) DESIGNER: JASON GÓMEZ
ART DIRECTOR: BEN GRAHAM  10. CLIENT: HANDI MEDICAL FIRM: CAPSULE (USA) DESIGNER: GREG BROSE ART DIRECTOR: BRIAN ADDUCCI
11. CLIENT: SWISSLIFE FIRM: METADESIGN (SWITZERLAND) DESIGNER: ANDRÉ STAUFFER ART DIRECTOR: ANDRÉ STAUFFER  12. CLIENT: COMPELLENT
FIRM: CAPSULE (USA) DESIGNER: DAN BAGGENSTOSS ART DIRECTOR: BRIAN ADDUCCI

1.

2.

3.

4.

AYRIN

5.

6.

1. CLIENT: INCOGNITO SUM FIRM: OCTAVO DESIGN PTY LTD (AUSTRALIA) DESIGNER: GARY DOMONEY ART DIRECTOR: GARY DOMONEY

2. CLIENT: DESIGN ASYLUM FIRM: DESIGN ASYLUM, INC. (USA) DESIGNER: LOWELL GILLIA ART DIRECTOR: LOWELL GILLIA 3. CLIENT: ELEMENT FIRM: ELEMENT (USA) DESIGNER: JEREMY SLAGLE, JOHN MCCOLLUM ART DIRECTOR: JEREMY SLAGLE 4. CLIENT: DAS BÜRO FIRM: KLAUS WILHARDT (DENMARK) DESIGNER: KLAUS WILHARDT ART DIRECTOR: KLAUS WILHARDT 5. CLIENT: AYRIN FIRM: JAN SABACH DESIGN (USA) DESIGNER: JAN SABACH ART DIRECTOR: JAN SABACH 6. CLIENT: CORBIS FIRM: SEGURA, INC. (USA) DESIGNER: THOP WONGSILLAPAKUN ART DIRECTOR: CARLOS SEGURA

7.

8.

9.

10.

11.

12.

7. CLIENT: WUNDERBURG DESIGN FIRM: WUNDERBURG DESIGN (GERMANY) DESIGNER: THOMAS FABIAN ART DIRECTOR: THOMAS FABIAN

8 CLIENT: 3 FIRM: 3 (USA) DESIGNER: TIM MCGRATH ART DESIGNER: SAM MACLAY 9. CLIENT: KAPSÜL PHOTOGRAPHY FIRM: AYSE ÇELEM DESIGN

(TURKEY) DESIGNER: AYSE ÇELEM ART DIRECTOR: AYSE ÇELEM 10. CLIENT: CUBE³ DEVELOPERS FIRM: OCTAVO DESIGN PTY LTD (AUSTRALIA)

DESIGNER: GARY DOMONEY ART DIRECTOR: GARY DOMONEY 11. CLIENT: GOGO IMAGE FIRM: SEGURA, INC. (USA) DESIGNERS: CHRIS MAY,

KIM HUBER ART DIRECTOR: CARLOS SEGURA 12. CLIENT: TIMBER DESIGN COMPANY FIRM: TIMBER DESIGN COMPANY, INC. (USA) DESIGNER:

LARS LAWSON ART DIRECTOR: LARS LAWSON

1.

2.

3.

4.

5.

6.

1. CLIENT: BERG COMMUNICATIONS FIRM: ANDREA EGBERT (USA) DESIGNER: ANDREA EGBERT ART DIRECTOR: ANDREA EGBERT 2. CLIENT: SPLENDID COMMUNICATIONS FIRM: CRUSH DESIGN (UK) DESIGNER: CHRIS PELLING ART DIRECTOR: CARL RUSH 3. CLIENT: VOICE FIRM: VOICE (AUSTRALIA) DESIGNER: SCOTT CARSLAKE ART DIRECTORS: SCOTT CARSLAKE, ANTHONY DE LEO 4. CLIENT: RENETTO FIRM: ELEMENT (USA) DESIGNERS: JEREMY SLAGLE, JOHN MCCOLLUM, PAUL ROBINETT ART DIRECTOR: JEREMY SLAGLE 5. CLIENT: HAPPY CAPITALIST FIRM: AYSE ÇELEM DESIGN (TURKEY) DESIGNER: AYSE ÇELEM ART DIRECTOR: AYSE ÇELEM 6. CLIENT: MIXER FIRM: MIXER (SWITZERLAND) DESIGNER: ERICH BRECHBÜHL ART DIRECTOR: ERICH BRECHBÜHL

7.

8.

9.

10.

11.

12.

7. CLIENT: PHOTOMOB FIRM: TURNSTYLE (USA) DESIGNERS: STEVE WATSON, JASON GÓMEZ ART DIRECTORS: JOHN BIELENBERG, STEVE WATSON

8. CLIENT: JOE SCHAAK FIRM: SUSSNER DESIGN COMPANY (USA) DESIGNER: BRANDON VAN LIERE ART DIRECTOR: DEREK SUSSNER

9. CLIENT: HUNGARIAN DESIGN COUNCIL FIRM: CSORDIZÁJN (HUNGARY) DESIGNER: ZOLTÁN CSORDÁS ART DIRECTOR: ZOLTÁN CSORDÁS

10. CLIENT: LIVADA FIRM: BRANDOCTOR (CROATIA) DESIGNER: SINISA SUDAR ART DIRECTOR: SINISA SUDAR 11. CLIENT: DELCARMEN

FIRM: SONSOLES LLORENS (SPAIN) DESIGNER: SONSOLES LLORENS ART DIRECTOR: SONSOLES LLORENS 12. CLIENT: VYWAY FIRM: NITA B.

CREATIVE (USA) DESIGNER: RENITA BREITENBUCHER ART DIRECTOR: RENITA BREITENBUCHER

1.

2.

3.

4.

5.

6.

1. CLIENT: SNAP PEA FIRM: CAPSULE (USA) DESIGNER: HEATHER WEISS ART DIRECTOR: BRIAN ADDUCCI  2. CLIENT: RANCHER'S CLUB
FIRM: RICKABAUGH GRAPHICS (USA) DESIGNER: ERIC RICKABAUGH ART DIRECTOR: ERIC RICKABAUGH  3. CLIENT: THRESHERS
FIRM: STERLING BRANDS (USA) DESIGNER: MARCUS HEWITT ART DIRECTOR: MARCUS HEWITT  4. CLIENT: ELENOV WINES FIRM: JELENA
DROBAC (SERBIA) DESIGNER: JELENA DROBAC ART DIRECTOR: JELENA DROBAC  5. CLIENT: TICKLE FISH FIRM: URBAN INFLUENCE DESIGN
STUDIO (USA) DESIGNER: HENRY YIU ART DIRECTOR: HENRY YIU  6. CLIENT: WAYZATA BAY SPICE COMPANY FIRM: CAPSULE (USA)
DESIGNER: BRIAN ADDUCCI ART DIRECTOR: BRIAN ADDUCCI

7.

8.

9.

10.

11.

12.

7. CLIENT: CARMARTHENSHIRE CHEESE COMPANY FIRM: FBA (WALES) DESIGNER: CHARLOTTE EDWARDS ART DIRECTOR: MEIRION WYN JONES
8. CLIENT: OLD NASSAU IMPORTS FIRM: CAPSULE (USA) DESIGNER: BRIAN ADDUCCI ART DIRECTOR: BRIAN ADDUCCI 9. CLIENT: EIGHT FIRM: HOLLIS
BRAND COMMUNICATIONS (USA) DESIGNER: DON HOLLIS ART DIRECTOR: DON HOLLIS 10. CLIENT: CAFÉ FINA FLOR FIRM: HARDY DESIGN (BRAZIL)
DESIGNERS: ANDREÁ GOMES, CAROLINA MARINI, MARIANA HARDY ART DIRECTOR: MARIANA HARDY 11. CLIENT: WORLD VIEW CAFE FIRM: ROME AND
GOLD CREATIVE (USA) DESIGNER: ROBERT E. GOLDIE ART DIRECTOR: LORENZO ROMERO 12. CLIENT: BLISSCOTTI FIRM: HORNALL ANDERSON DESIGN
WORKS (USA) DESIGNERS: LARRY ANDERSON, HOLLY CRAVEN, JAY HILBURN, CHRIS FREED ART DIRECTORS: LARRY ANDERSON, JACK ANDERSON

1.

2.

3.

4.

5.

6.

1. CLIENT: PAPOU'S GREEK CAFE & TAVERNA FIRM: SQUIRES & COMPANY (USA) DESIGNER: GARRETT OWEN ART DIRECTOR: BRANDON MURPHY
2. CLIENT: ENOTRIA WINECELLARS, LTD. FIRM: SOCIAL (UK) DESIGNER: PAUL DRIVER ART DIRECTOR: PAUL DRIVER 3. CLIENT: LUND FOOD HOLDINGS
FIRM: CAPSULE (USA) DESIGNER: BRIAN ADDUCCI ART DIRECTOR: BRIAN ADDUCCI 4. CLIENT: THE HOUSE OF BRICKS FIRM: SAYLES GRAPHIC DESIGN
(USA) DESIGNER: JOHN SAYLES ART DIRECTOR: JOHN SAYLES 5. CLIENT: DON JOAQUIN FIRM: GEYRHALTER DESIGN (USA) DESIGNERS: EVELYN KIM,
JOHN TSAI ART DIRECTOR: FABIAN GEYRHALTER 6. CLIENT: SNACKWISE FIRM: LLOYDS GRAPHIC DESIGN (NEW ZEALAND) DESIGNER: ALEXANDER
LLOYD ART DIRECTOR: ALEXANDER LLOYD

# DOWNTOWNER
-WOODFIRE GRILLE-

7.

8.

9.

10.

11.

12.

7. CLIENT: DOWNTOWNER FIRM: CAPSULE (USA) DESIGNER: BRIAN ADDUCCI ART DIRECTOR: BRIAN ADDUCCI  8. CLIENT: WONDER BAR
FIRM: WOLKEN COMMUNICA (USA) DESIGNERS: JOHANN GOMEZ, RYAN BURLINSON ART DIRECTOR: KURT WOLKEN  9. CLIENT: CALIFORNIA
BARBECUE ASSOCIATION FIRM: CHRIS ROONEY ILLUSTRATION/DESIGN (USA) DESIGNER: CHRIS ROONEY ART DIRECTOR: CHRIS ROONEY
10. CLIENT: FALLON AND BYRNE FIRM: THE PARTNERS (UK) DESIGNERS: KERRY OSTERMEYER, MIKE PRATLEY ART DIRECTORS: GREG QUINTON,
JIM PRIOR  11. CLIENT: EDWARDS FIRM: MICHAEL THIELE (GERMANY) DESIGNER: MICHAEL THIELE ART DIRECTOR: MICHAEL THIELE
12. CLIENT: SEAFOOD COOKING SCHOOL FIRM: LLOYDS GRAPHIC DESIGN LTD (NEW ZEALAND) DESIGNER: ALEXANDER LLOYD
ART DIRECTOR: ALEXANDER LLOYD

THE ESDAILES

1.

2.

3.

MUSICAPOLIS

4.

HYPE ™

5.

WatchNetwork.com

6.

1. CLIENT: CHARLES ESDAILE FIRM: ALPHABET ARM DESIGN (USA) DESIGNER: AARON BELYEA ART DIRECTOR: AARON BELYEA 2. CLIENT: TNN FIRM: SEGURA, INC. (USA) DESIGNERS: AKARIT LEEYAVANICH, ANISA SUTHAYALAI, DAVE WEIK ART DIRECTOR: CARLOS SEGURA 3. CLIENT: EVOLUTION RECORDS FIRM: A3 DESIGN (USA) DESIGNER: AMANDA ALTMAN ART DIRECTOR: ALAN ALTMAN 4. CLIENT: MCP-MUSICAPOLIS FIRM: GRAPHICULTURE (USA) DESIGNERS: DANIEL ANDERSON, CHAD OLSON, LINDSEY GICE 5. CLIENT: HYPE MAGAZINE FIRM: ROCHOLL SELECTED DESIGNS (GERMANY) DESIGNER: FRANK ROCHOLL ART DIRECTOR: FRANK ROCHOLL 6. CLIENT: WATCHNETWORK.COM FIRM: PENTAGRAM DESIGN (USA) DESIGNER: WOODY PIRTLE ART DIRECTOR: WOODY PIRTLE

7.

8.

9.

10.

11.

12.

7. CLIENT: BRIAN APPEL/THE BOSTON PHOENIX FIRM: ALPHABET ARM DESIGN (USA) DESIGNER: DAVE WALL ART DIRECTOR: AARON BELYEA

8. CLIENT: FINE LINE FEATURES FIRM: PENTAGRAM DESIGN (USA) DESIGNER: WOODY PIRTLE ART DIRECTOR: WOODY PIRTLE 9. CLIENT: SCOTT &

SCOTT DIRECTORS FIRM: DEE DELARA DESIGNER: DEE DELARA (USA) ART DIRECTOR: DEE DELARA 10. CLIENT: DÜSSELDORFER SCHAUSPIELHAUS

FIRM: LIGALUX GMBH (GERMANY) DESIGNERS: MARTIN SCHWATLO, HANA SEDELMAYER ART DIRECTORS: PETRA MATOUSCHEK, MARTINA MASSONG

11. CLIENT: HUMAN PLC FIRM: SOCIAL (UK) DESIGNER: PAUL DRIVER ART DIRECTOR: PAUL DRIVER 12. CLIENT: POST PUNK KITCHEN FIRM: ALR DESIGN

(USA) DESIGNER: NOAH SCALIN ART DIRECTOR: NOAH SCALIN

1.

2.

3.

4.

5.

6.

1. CLIENT: RADIO RANCH FIRM: PENTAGRAM DESIGN (USA) DESIGNER: WOODY PIRTLE ART DIRECTOR: WOODY PIRTLE  2. CLIENT: KAY HANLEY AND MICHELLE LEWIS FIRM: ALPHABET ARM DESIGN (USA) DESIGNER: AARON BELYEA ART DIRECTOR: AARON BELYEA  3. CLIENT: AMI MAGAZINE FIRM: ROCHOLL SELECTED DESIGNS (GERMANY) DESIGNER: JORGE GEBAUHR ART DIRECTOR: FRANK ROCHOLL  4. CLIENT: CATLICK RECORDS FIRM: FAUXKOI DESIGN COMPANY (USA) DESIGNER: DAN WEST ART DIRECTOR: DAN WEST  5. CLIENT: C31 (CHANNEL 31) FIRM: OCTAVO DESIGN PTY LTD (AUSTRALIA) DESIGNER: GARY DOMONEY ART DIRECTOR: GARY DOMONEY  6. CLIENT: SHANNON O'ROURKE FIRM: SPECIAL MODERN DESIGN (USA) DESIGNER: KAREN BARRANCO ART DIRECTOR: KAREN BARRANCO

7.

8.

9.

10.

11.

12.

7. CLIENT: MALAB FIRM: HARDY DESIGN (BRAZIL) DESIGNERS: GUSTAVO GRECCO, ROBERTO BELLINI, MARIANA HARDY ART DIRECTOR: MARIANA HARDY

8. CLIENT: F-FIVE FIRM: UNIT-Y (USA) DESIGNER: ANDREY NAGORNY ART DIRECTOR: ANDREY NAGORNY  9. CLIENT: MAROON 5 FIRM: MATTSON CREATIVE

(USA) DESIGNER: TY MATTSON ART DIRECTOR: TY MATTSON  10. CLIENT: ZENCAST FIRM: GLITSCHKA STUDIOS (USA) DESIGNER: VON R. GLITSCHKA

ART DIRECTOR: VON R. GLITSCHKA  11. CLIENT: HOT SAKÉ CREATIVE FIRM: A3 DESIGN (USA) DESIGNER: AMANDA ALTMAN ART DIRECTOR: ALAN ALTMAN

12. CLIENT: JDUB RECORDS FIRM: ALPHABET ARM DESIGN (USA) DESIGNER: RYAN FREASE ART DIRECTOR: AARON BELYEA

1.

2.

3.

4.

5.

6.

KARL BRÖCKER STIFTUNG

ZUKUNFT FÜR KINDER

7.

8.

9.

10.

11.

12.

7. CLIENT: KARL BRÖCKER STIFTUNG FIRM: MICHAEL THIELE DESIGNER: MICHAEL THIELE ART DIRECTOR: MICHAEL THIELE 8. CLIENT: PUSH INSTITUTE FIRM: CAPSULE (USA) DESIGNER: GREG BROSE ART DIRECTOR: BRIAN ADDUCCI 9. CLIENT: NEBRASKA AIDS PROJECT FIRM: OXIDE DESIGN COMPANY (USA) DESIGNERS: DREW DAVIES, JOE SPARANO ART DIRECTOR: DREW DAVIES 10. CLIENT: CASA DOS ESPÍRITOS EDITORA FIRM: ANDREI POLESSI-GRAFIKZ (BRAZIL) DESIGNER: ANDREI POLESSI ART DIRECTOR: ANDREI POLESSI 11. CLIENT: ANGLO AMERICAN FIRM: THE PARTNERS (UK) DESIGNERS: ANNABEL CLEMENTS, ESTHER RUSHTON, DAVID RICHARDS, IAN LANKSBURY ART DIRECTOR: JAMES BEVERAGE 12. CLIENT: MYTOWN, INC. FIRM: COLLABORATED, INC. (USA) DESIGNER: JAMES EVELOCK ART DIRECTOR: JAMES EVELOCK

1.

2.

3.

4.

MODCOM

5.

6.

1. CLIENT: ALLBALL INC. FIRM: D4 CREATIVE GROUP (USA) DESIGNER: WICKY WAI-KUEN LEE ART DIRECTOR: WICKY WAI-KUEN LEE 2. CLIENT: FREE LIBRARY OF PHILADELPHIA FIRM: SIEGEL & GALE (USA) DESIGNER: DANIEL A. JOHNSTON ART DIRECTOR: HOWARD BELK 3. CLIENT: ROAD RASH NATIONALS FIRM: OXIDE DESIGN COMPANY (USA) DESIGNERS: DREW DAVIES, JOE SPARANO ART DIRECTOR: DREW DAVIES 4. CLIENT: ROBERT WOOD JOHNSON FOUNDATION FIRM: SIEGEL & GALE (USA) DESIGNER: YOUNG KIM ART DIRECTOR: HOWARD BELK 5. CLIENT: LOS ANGELES CONSERVANCY MODERN COMMITTEE FIRM: SPECIAL MODERN DESIGN (USA) DESIGNER: KAREN BARRANCO ART DIRECTOR: KAREN BARRANCO 6. CLIENT: FRESH ENERGY FIRM: CAPSULE (USA) DESIGNER: GREG BROSE ART DIRECTOR: BRIAN ADDUCCI

7.

8.

9.

10.

11.

12.

7. CLIENT: LINCOLN PARKS AND REC FOUNDATION FIRM: AIJALON (USA) DESIGNER: LANCE FORD ART DIRECTOR: LANCE FORD 8. CLIENT: AWESOME WOMEN FIRM: CAPSULE (USA) DESIGNER: HEATHER WEISS ART DIRECTOR: BRIAN ADDUCCI 9. CLIENT: HOMES WITH HEART FOSTER FAMILY AGENCY FIRM: EWERT DESIGN (USA) DESIGNER: VINCE EWERT ART DIRECTOR: VINCE EWERT 10. CLIENT: KARIM RIDA SAID FOUNDATION FIRM: LOEWY (UK) DESIGNER: PAUL BURGESS ART DIRECTOR: PAUL BURGESS 11. CLIENT: FERNDALE PUBLIC LIBRARY FIRM: IDEATION SIGNS & COMMUNICATIONS, INC. (USA) DESIGNER: EVAN ROATH ART DIRECTOR: KACHA AZÉMA 12. CLIENT: BLOKHAUS/GRAHAM DOWNES ARCHITECTURE FIRM: HOLLIS BRAND COMMUNICATIONS (USA) DESIGNER: DON HOLLIS ART DIRECTOR: DON HOLLIS

1.

2.

3.

4.

5.

6.

1. CLIENT: VENUE FIRM: TURNSTYLE (USA) DESIGNER: BEN GRAHAM ART DIRECTOR: BEN GRAHAM  2. CLIENT: 3M COMPANY FIRM: WALLACE CHURCH, INC. (USA) DESIGNER: HEATHER ALLEN ART DIRECTOR: STAN CHURCH  3. CLIENT: HS FASHION/CASUÉ FIRM: SIMON AND GOETZ DESIGN (GERMANY) DESIGNER: GERRIT HINKELBEIN ART DIRECTOR: PIA KEMPTER  4. CLIENT: B&BEYOND FIRM: RAMP (USA) DESIGNER: MICHAEL STINSON ART DIRECTORS: MICHAEL STINSON, RACHEL ELNAR  5. CLIENT: THE PALACE FIRM: S & N DESIGN (USA) DESIGNER: STEVE LEE ART DIRECTOR: STEVE LEE  6. CLIENT: YANK FIRM: CAPSULE (USA) DESIGNER: BRIAN ADDUCCI ART DIRECTOR: BRIAN ADDUCCI

Urban
**industries**

7.

Spoylt

8.

LUXI

9.

meangirl

10.

SCREAMER

11.

clover™

12.

7. CLIENT: URBAN INDUSTRIES FIRM: URBAN INFLUENCE DESIGN STUDIO (USA) DESIGNERS: MICHAEL MATES, HENRY YIU ART DIRECTOR: HENRY YIU
8. CLIENT: SPOYLT FIRM: PEARLFISHER (UK) DESIGNER: KEELEY COUSINS ART DIRECTOR: KAREN WELMAN 9. CLIENT: LUXI FIRM: LISKA + ASSOCIATES
(USA) DESIGNER: JONATHAN SEEDS ART DIRECTOR: TANYA QUICK 10. CLIENT: MEAN GIRL FIRM: DESIGN RANCH (USA) DESIGNERS: MICHELLE
SONDEREGGER, INGRED SIDIE ART DIRECTORS: MICHELLE SONDEREGGER, INGRED SIDIE 11. CLIENT: SCREAMER HATS FIRM: HORNALL ANDERSON
DESIGN WORKS (USA) DESIGNERS: KATHY SAITO, SONJA MAX ART DIRECTOR: KATHY SAITO 12. CLIENT: CLOVER FIRM: TURNSTYLE (USA)
DESIGNER: JASON GÓMEZ ART DIRECTOR: BEN GRAHAM

cottons

1.

2.

chunk

3.

4.

UB OUTFITTERS

5.

6.

1. CLIENT: COTTONS FIRM: SPARK STUDIO PTY LTD (AUSTRALIA) DESIGNER: SEAN PETHICK ART DIRECTOR: SEAN PETHICK  2. CLIENT: COMPASS MARKETING FIRM: CAPSULE (USA) DESIGNER: BRIAN ADDUCCI ART DIRECTOR: BRIAN ADDUCCI  3. CLIENT: TAKEMON GAMES PTY LTD FIRM: VOICE (AUSTRALIA) DESIGNER: SCOTT CARSLAKE ART DIRECTOR: SCOTT CARSLAKE  4. CLIENT: CHUNK FIRM: SOCIAL (UK) DESIGNER: PAUL DRIVER ART DIRECTOR: PAUL DRIVER  5. CLIENT: UNION BAY OUTFITTERS FIRM: GLITSCHKA STUDIOS (USA) DESIGNER: VON R. GLITSCHKA ART DIRECTOR: VON R. GLITSCHKA  6. CLIENT: BRAINCANDY FIRM: TURNSTYLE (USA) DESIGNER: STEVE WATSON ART DIRECTOR: STEVE WATSON

7.

8.

9.

10.

P A N T E A S E™

11.

12.

7. CLIENT: MAX RAVE LLC FIRM: MICHAEL OSBORNE DESIGN (USA) DESIGNER: MICHAEL OSBORNE ART DIRECTOR: MICHAEL OSBORNE  8. CLIENT: JUA KALI FIRM: MIND CORPORATION (UK) DESIGNER: ANDREW KING ART DIRECTOR: ANDREW ROBINSON  9. CLIENT: CARDRAGEOUS FIRM: BBDK, INC. (USA) DESIGNER: DUANE KING ART DIRECTOR: DUANE KING 10. CLIENT: MOODY BLUES, A DENIM SOCIETY FIRM: NOCTURNAL GRAPHIC DESIGN STUDIO (USA) DESIGNER: KEN PETERS ART DIRECTOR: KEN PETERS 11. CLIENT: EQUIS FIRM: SPIL CREATIVE, INC. (USA) DESIGNERS: DAMIAN DOMINGUEZ, JIEUN LEE ART DIRECTORS: DAMIAN DOMINGUEZ, JIEUN LEE 12. CLIENT: PANTEASE FIRM: DESIGN RANCH (USA) DESIGNER: MICHELLE SONDEREGGER ART DIRECTORS: MICHELLE SONDEREGGER,  INGRED SIDIE

# CONTRE

# BUTORS

FOR ME, IT'S THAT I CONTRIBUTED…THAT I'M ON THIS PLANET DOING SOME GOOD AND MAKING PEOPLE HAPPY. THAT'S TO ME THE MOST IMPORTANT THING.
– ELLEN DEGENERES

**A3 DESIGN**
USA
www.athreedesign.com

Page 172
Art Director: Alan Altman
Designer: Amanda Altman
Client: Evolution Records

Page 152
Art Director: Alan Altman
Designer: Amanda Altman
Client: Goodys Paint Company

Page 175
Art Director: Alan Altman
Designer: Amanda Altman
Client: Hot Saké Creative

**ADSOKA**
Page 155
Art Director: Gretchen
Westbrock
Designer: Gretchen Westbrock
Client: Mendota Homes
USA
www.adsoka.com

**AIJALON**
USA
www.aijalon.net

Page 154
Art Director: Lance Ford
Designer: Jill Andreasen
Client: Guinco

Page 179
Art Director: Lance Ford
Designer: Lance Ford
Client: Lincoln Parks and Rec
Foundation

**ALPHABET ARM DESIGN**
USA
www.alphabetarm.com

Page 173
Art Director: Aaron Belyea
Designer: Dave Wall
Client: Brian Appel/The Boston
Phoenix

Page 172
Art Director: Aaron Belyea
Designer: Aaron Belyea
Client: Charles Esdaile

Page 174
Art Director: Aaron Belyea
Designer: Aaron Belyea
Client: Kay Hanley and Michelle
Lewis

Page 175
Art Director: Aaron Belyea
Designer: Ryan Frease
Client: Jdub Records

**ALR DESIGN**
Page 173
Art Director: Noah Scalin
Designer: Noah Scalin
Client: Post Punk Kitchen
USA
www.alrdesign.com

**ANDREI POLESSI
– GRAFIKZ**
Page 177
Art Director: Andrei Polessi
Designer: Andrei Polessi
Client: Casa dos Espíritos
Editora
Brazil
www.grafikz.com

**AYSE ÇELEM DESIGN**
Turkey
www.aysecelemdesign.com

Page 166
Art Director: Ayse Çelem
Designer: Ayse Çelem
Client: Happy Capitalist

Page 165
Art Director: Ayse Çelem
Designer: Ayse Çelem
Client: Kapsül Photography

**BASS & YAGER**
Page 24
Art Director: Saul Bass
Client: AT&T

**BBDK, INC.**
Page 183
Art Director: Duane King
Designer: Duane King
Client: Cardrageous
USA
www.bbdk.com

**BOHNSACK DESIGN**
Page 176
Art Director: Chris Bohnsack
Designer: Chris Bohnsack
Client: The Phoenix Symphony,
Le Masquerade Ball
USA
www.bohnsackdesign.com

**BRANDOCTOR**
Page 167
Art Director: Siniša Sudar
Designer: Siniša Sudar
Client: Livada
Croatia
www.brandoctor.com

**CAPSULE**
USA
www.capsule.us

Page 160
Art Director: Brian Adducci
Designer: Dan Baggenstoss
Client: Animal Adventure

Page 179
Art Director: Brian Adducci
Designer: Heather Weiss
Client: Awesome Women

Page 45
Art Director: Brian Adducci
Designer: Brian Adducci
Client: Buck 'n' Jims

Page 158
Art Director: Brian Adducci
Designer: Dan Baggenstoss
Client: Burlwood Financial
Group, Inc.

Page 64
Art Director: Brian Adducci
Designer: Brian Adducci
Client: Cerenity

Page 182
Art Director: Brian Adducci
Designer: Brian Adducci
Client: Compass Marketing

Page 163
Art Director: Brian Adducci
Designer: Dan Baggenstoss
Client: Compellent

Page 171
Art Director: Brian Adducci
Designer: Brian Adducci
Client: Downtowner Woodfire
Grille

Page 87
Art Director: Brian Adducci
Designer: Brian Adducci
Client: Experience Engineering

Page 43
Art Director: Brian Adducci
Designer: Greg Brose
Client: Fox River Mills, Inc.

Page 178
Art Director: Brian Adducci
Designer: Greg Brose
Client: Fresh Energy

Page 159
Art Director: Brian Adducci
Designer: Dan Baggenstoss
Client: Gatorback

Page 39, 54
Art Director: Brian Adducci
Designer: Brian Adducci
Client: Gear6

Page 69
Art Director: Brian Adducci
Designer: Anchalee
Chambundabongse
Client: Goodnight Moon

Page 163
Art Director: Brian Adducci
Designer: Greg Brose
Client: Handi Medical

Page 86
Art Director: Brian Adducci
Designer: Brian Adducci
Client: Jackal Open

Page 118
Art Director: Brian Adducci
Designers: Greg Brose, Brian
Adducci
Client: Lund Food Holdings

Page 32, 33, 34, 35
Art Director: Brian Adducci
Designer: Greg Brose
Client: Myth Night Club

Page 169
Art Director: Brian Adducci
Designer: Brian Adducci
Client: Old Nassau Imports

Page 161
Art Director: Brian Adducci
Designer: Dan Baggenstoss
Client: Paladin

Page 19
Art Director: Brian Adducci
Designer: Brian Adducci
Client: PrairieStone Pharmacy

Page 177
Art Director: Brian Adducci
Designer: Greg Brose
Client: The Push Institute

Page 61, 126, 127, 128, 129
Art Director: Brian Adducci
Designer: Dan Baggenstoss
Client: Red Wing Shoe
Company, Inc.

Page 168
Art Director: Brian Adducci
Designer: Heather Weiss
Client: Snap Pea

Page 102
Art Director: Brian Adducci
Designer: Dan Baggenstoss
Client: The Society of American
Fight Directors

Page 162
Art Director: Brian Adducci
Designer: Heather Weiss
Client: Survey and Ballot
Systems

Page 94, 95
Art Director: Brian Adducci
Designer: Ola Supernat
Client: 3Wire

Page 154
Art Director: Brian Adducci
Designer: Dan Baggenstoss
Client: Urban Blueprint

Page 168
Art Director: Brian Adducci
Designer: Brian Adducci
Client: Wayzata Bay Spice
Company

Page 79
Art Director: Brian Adducci
Designer: Greg Brose
Client: WineHaven

Page 107
Art Director: Brian Adducci
Designer: Dan Baggenstoss
Client: Worx

Page 180
Art Director: Brian Adducci
Designer: Brian Adducci
Client: Yank

**CC GRAPHIC DESIGN**
Page 62
Art Director: Carolyn Crowley
Designer: Carolyn Crowley
Client: The Children's Museum
of Utah
USA
www.ccgraphicdesignstudio.
com

**CDI STUDIOS**
Page 62
Art Director: Dan McElhattan III
Designer: Dan McElhattan III
Client: Osaka Sushi Bar Logo
USA
www.cdistudios.com

**CEMSTONE PRODUCTS
COMPANY**
Page 75
www.cemstone.com

**CHRIS ROONEY
ILLUSTRATION/DESIGN**
Page 171
Art Director: Chris Rooney
Designer: Chris Rooney
Client: California Barbecue
Association
USA
www.looneyrooney.com

**TIMBER DESIGN COMPANY, INC.**
USA
www.timberdesignco.com

Page 176
Art Director: Lars Lawson
Designer: Lars Lawson
Client: Indiana Urban Forest Council

Page 165
Art Director: Lars Lawson
Designer: Lars Lawson
Client: Timber Design Company

**TOTAL IDENTITY BV**
The Netherlands
www.totalidentity.nl

Page 157
Art Director: André Mol
Designer: André Mol
Client: De Ruiter

Page 162
Art Director: André Mol
Designer: André Mol
Client: Hanaro Telecom

Page 156
Art Director: Léon Stolk
Designer: Léon Stolk
Client: Oasen

**TURNSTYLE**
USA
www.turnstylestudio.com

Page 182
Art Director: Steve Watson
Designer: Steve Watson
Client: Braincandy

Page 181
Art Director: Ben Graham
Designer: Jason Gómez
Client: Clover

Page 43
Art Director: Steve Watson
Designer: Steve Watson
Client: DRY Soda Company

Page 158
Art Director: Ben Graham
Designer: Ben Graham
Client: Mpire

Page 163
Art Director: Ben Graham
Designer: Jason Gómez
Client: Parametric

Page 167 ·
Art Directors: John Bielenberg,
Steve Watson
Designers: Steve Watson, Jason Gómez
Client: Photomob

Page 180
Art Director: Ben Graham
Designer: Ben Graham
Client: Venue

**28 LIMITED BRAND**
Germany
www.twenty-eight.de

Page 161
Art Director: Mirco Kurth
Designer: Mirco Kurth
Client: Dr. Koepchen

Page 160
Art Director: Mirco Kurth
Designer: Mirco Kurth
Client: Systemtrans

**UNIT-Y**
USA
www.unit-y.com

Page 156
Art Director: Andrey Nagorny
Designer: Andrey Nagorny
Client: Bagby and Company

Page 175
Art Director: Andrey Nagorny
Designer: Andrey Nagorny
Client: F-Five

**URBAN INFLUENCE DESIGN
STUDIO**
USA
www.urbaninfluence.com

Page 156
Art Director: Henry Yiu
Designers: Michael Mates, Henry Yiu
Client: 59 Limousine

Page 168
Art Director: Henry Yiu
Designer: Henry Yiu
Client: Tickle Fish

Page 181
Art Director: Henry Yiu
Designers: Michael Mates, Henry Yiu
Client: Urban Industries

Page 155
Art Director: Henry Yiu
Designer: Michael Mates, Henry Yiu
Client: Wags

**VOICE**
Australia
www.voicedesign.net

Page 182
Art Director: Scott Carslake
Designer: Scott Carslake
Client: Takemon Games Pty Ltd

Page 166
Art Directors: Scott Carslake, Anthony
de Leo
Designer: Scott Carslake
Client: Voice

**WALLACE CHURCH, INC.**
Page 180
Art Director: Stan Church
Designer: Heather Allen
Client: 3M Company
USA
www.wallacechurch.com

**WHITERHINO**
Page 162
Art Director: Andrew Tibb
Designer: Andrew Tibb, Jeremy Tibb,
Peter Binek
Client: Coronet
Australia
www.whiterhino.com.au

**KLAUS WILHARDT**
Page 164
Art Director: Klaus Wilhardt
Designer: Klaus Wilhardt
Client: Das Büro / Photographers
Denmark

**WOLFF OLINS**
USA
www.wolff-olins.com

Page 77
Art Directors: Doug Selters, Adam Throup
Designers: Henncus Kusbianto, Andrew
Wilson, Michael Lin
Client: General Electric

Page 60
Art Director: Todd Simmons
Designer: Lily Williams
Client: Make (formerly, Our Name Is Mud)

Page 29
Art Director: Sam Wilson
Designers: Andrew Wilson, Bethany Koby
Client: Smith & Nephew

Page 146, 147, 148, 149
Art Director: Karl Heiselman
Designers: Todd Simmons, Sam Wilson,
Christian Butte, JP Chirdow, Sebastian
Klein
Client: (RED)

**WOLKEN COMMUNICA**
USA
www.wolkencommunica.com

Page 154
Art Director: Kurt Wolken
Designer: Ryan Burlinson
Client: Emazement

Page 171
Art Director: Kurt Wolken
Designer: Johann Gomez, Ryan Burlinson
Client: Wonder Bar

**WUNDERBURG DESIGN**
Page 165
Art Director: Thomas Fabian
Designer: Thomas Fabian
Client: Wunderburg Design
Germany
www.wunderburg-design.de

**Y&R**
Page 159
Art Director: Chris Rooney
Designer: Chris Rooney
Client: RadarGolf
USA
www.sfo.yr.com

# About Capsule

Capsule develops local, national, and international brands from its nerve center in the heart of Minneapolis, Minnesota, USA. Its mission is to reduce the risk of taking brands, products, and services to market through qualitative research methods, holistic brand strategy, comprehensive identity systems, memorable naming, package and experience design, and creative writing solutions.

Capsule was founded by Brian Adducci, a designer whose brand and identity expertise is sought by international clients, and Aaron Keller, an adjunct professor of marketing at the University of St. Thomas. Their firm houses an eclectic collection of designers, managers, lawyers, writers, and researchers.

Clients include Fisher-Price, Honeywell, Red Wing Shoes, Target, Sally Hansen, Net Gear, Capital One, Medtronic, Panda Express, and Cargill.

CAPSULE
10 South 5th Street, Suite 645
Minneapolis, Minnesota 55402
USA

www.capsule.us

612-341-4525
info@capsule.us